ART DECO TEXTILES

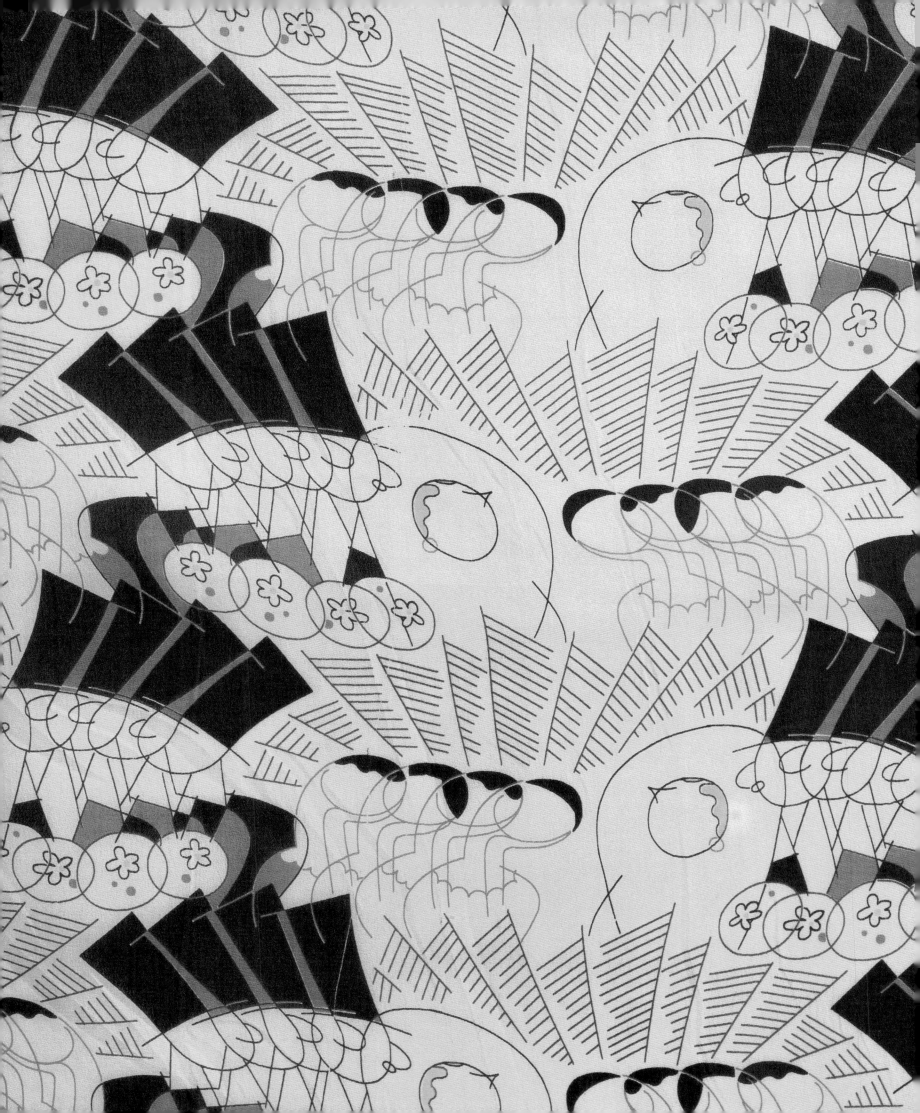

ART DECO TEXTILES

CHARLOTTE SAMUELS

PHOTOGRAPHY BY CHRISTINE SMITH

V&A PUBLICATIONS

DISTRIBUTED BY HARRY N. ABRAMS, INC., PUBLISHERS

First published by V&A Publications, 2003

V&A Publications
160 Brompton Road
London
SW3 1HW

Distributed in North America by Harry N. Abrams, Incorporated,
New York

ISBN 0-8109-6604-2 (Harry N. Abrams, Inc)

Library of Congress Control Number 2002115665

Designed by Area

Photography by Christine Smith, V&A Photographic Studio

Front jacket illustration: *Surfers*, dress fabric (see plate 92)
Back jacket illustration: *Stars and Stripes*, dress fabric (see plate 64)
Frontispiece: *Gentlemen Prefer Blondes*, dress fabric (see plate 65)

Printed in Singapore

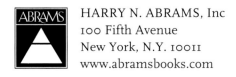
HARRY N. ABRAMS, Inc
100 Fifth Avenue
New York, N.Y. 10011
www.abramsbooks.com

Contents

Art Deco Textiles

Charlotte Samuels

Sources and Influences

Art Deco is a style that takes its name from the Exposition Internationale des Arts Décoratifs et Industriels Modernes, held in Paris in 1925. The term is a descriptive label given in retrospect to a range of decorative trends that span the years 1910 to 1940. The furnishing and dress textiles produced during these decades, particularly in France and the US, constitute an immediate visual record of the evolution of fashionable taste. Two distinct moments can be discerned within Art Deco: a formalized, ornamental style typical of French-produced goods; and the angular, abstract, streamlined look of American modern.

The dating of movements within the arts is always somewhat arbitrary, and it is possible to trace the development of Art Deco out of preceding stylistic tendencies encompassed by Art Nouveau. During the first decade of the twentieth century many designers sought to move away from the intricate, naturalistic forms characteristic of Art Nouveau. Revolutionary developments in the fine arts also greatly influenced the appearance of Art Deco. At the beginning of the twentieth century France was the centre of the art world and the most important innovation in painting was Cubism, a movement which challenged the mathematically exact one-point perspective dominant in Western art since the Renaissance. From about 1910 onwards the Cubists introduced a new conception of space which took the form of an angular and fragmented perspective. Artists such as Picasso drew inspiration from so-called primitive art and were fascinated by objects from non-Western cultures, among them African carvings and shields (plate 1).

Colour was another element that painters redeployed in a strikingly imaginative way. The Fauves juxtaposed shockingly bright hues to release the energy contained within colour. A new interest in Arab culture was sparked off by the French colonization of North African and Middle Eastern countries during the nineteenth century, and this taste for exoticism was sustained by Dr J.C. Mardrus's translation of *The Thousand and One Nights* (otherwise known as *The Arabian Nights*) into French at the turn of the century. Clothing and textiles of this provenance exerted a visible effect on the imagination of couturiers such as Paul Poiret.

Various historical sources also inspired the artists, designers and manufacturers responsible for producing Deco textiles. French furniture-makers were influenced by the elegant simplicity of the past, particularly late eighteenth-century neo-classicism and early nineteenth-century restraint. From creating expensive individual pieces, designers began to set up workshops in department stores which produced furniture in limited series; Paul Follot, for example, made items for Pomone at Au Bon Marché in Paris.

After the First World War there was greater social mobility, and this led to a change in domestic circumstances for many middle-class people. One consequence was that there were fewer servants, which meant the cost of home help increased. As a result, home owners opted for a plain, uncluttered living space. Technological improvements made central heating more widely available, and this permitted a flexible room layout. To save space, smaller pieces of furniture were produced, and some items such as wardrobes and shelves were built-in rather than free-standing. Designers began to create integrated environments in which the upholstery and wall, window and floor decorations all blended harmoniously.

Glowing colour was first popularized through its appearance in dress fabrics. Poiret, the most innovative fashion designer of his day, reshaped the female silhouette by clothing it in slim, Empire-line apparel derived from the late eighteenth century and the untailored shapes of Eastern garments. This fashion called for soft, fluid cloth which could be draped over the body, in contrast to the stiff, formal materials of the early twentieth century. The idea of a look that altered regularly came from clothing collections that changed each season, and stimulated the demand for new textiles. Many of the patrons who commissioned lavish Art Deco interiors were from the world of fashion, among them the couturiers Jeanne Lanvin, Madeleine Vionnet, Coco Chanel and Jacques Dunand.

A mixture of natural and synthetic materials was often used for the sake of durability, in both furnishing and dress fabrics. The most significant advance was the development and improvement of the rayon manufacturing process in the US. Initially marketed as 'artificial silk', rayon was disliked for its shiny appearance, which was thought to be cheap-looking. Attempts to invent a silk substitute had been ongoing since the nineteenth century, but the process was not perfected until the late 1920s, at which point rayon's adaptability was finally recognized. The raw material from which rayon is created is cellulose from wood pulp or cotton linters (fibres). This is spun into yarns whose thickness can be controlled so that a similar weight to silk, linen, cotton or even wool can be achieved. The degree of sheen can also be varied from matte to lustrous, and fabrics made from rayon are hard-wearing and easy to keep clean. Ninon, a gossamer-like material, was in vogue during the 1920s for sheer curtains. Rayon apparel was popularized by Schiaparelli who employed a textured crêpe variant in the early 1930s to make figure-hugging evening dresses which gave the wearer a sculptural outline. The comparatively low cost of producing synthetic fabric meant that it was sold inexpensively and by the mid-1930s, 85 per cent of dress fabrics sold in the US were made from rayon textiles.

The 1925 Exhibition

The 1925 Paris exhibition was a milestone in the history of textile and furnishing design, marking as it did the zenith of the French taste for luxurious goods ornamentally crafted from expensive materials. The participating nations, including most European countries, China and Japan, were allocated sites for the construction of temporary pavilions in which to array their exhibits.

The French hosts displayed the most outstanding examples of upholstery, drapery and dress fabrics. Some of their pavilions were erected by regional committees, such as the Pavillon de Lyon, which highlighted the products of the French textile industry, and in particular the work of Raoul Dufy. Others were sponsored by department stores such as Au Bon Marché. The exhibition space further comprised purpose-built boutiques, including an outlet selling Sonia Delaunay's 'simultaneous' abstract designs, and even three barges fitted out by Poiret to showcase the printed fabrics of his studio, Atelier Martine.

The aim of the exhibition was to display contemporary decorative art, focusing in particular on the modernity of its conception and style. The French promoted their status as leaders in the field of interior design, specializing in the production of entire rooms of co-ordinated furnishings which encompassed every element from carpets to hangings. Interestingly, neither Germany nor the US was involved in the exhibition, even though both nations were to be major contributors to the Modernist strain of Art Deco, which by the following decade would succeed the opulent French style of the 1920s.

German pre-eminence in the decorative arts early in the century stimulated the French to compete. In fact, the 1925 exhibition had originally been scheduled for 1915, but the First World War and its aftermath forced the postponement of the event. By the time the exhibition finally took place Germany could no longer participate, for both political and economic reasons. Leading Americans, meanwhile, did not believe the US could compete with Europe in the field of innovative, modern design at this time. This was despite the fact that the American skyscraper was one of the most avant-garde architectural forms of the era, whose streamlining was to shape the development of Art Deco.

Early Art Deco: Into Abstraction

Initial examples of the application of abstract representation in textile design can be seen in the work of Charles Rennie Mackintosh. A 1918 fabric incorporates a repeat of an elongated flower bud over a pulsing web of dark lines (plate 2). Exhibited in Austria, Italy and Germany, Mackintosh's work was associated with Art Nouveau and not generally appreciated in Britain. Yet his compositions inspired leading designers of the forward-looking Munich school and Joseph Hoffmann, head of the textile department at Austria's Wiener Werkstätte.

The Wiener Werkstätte was a guild of artists and craftsmen who came together with the aim of updating the ideals and style embodied by Art Nouveau, representing 'a European avant-garde and an aesthetic rather than a social response to the challenge of modernity'.[1] Hoffmann's restrained geometric tulips from 1910–11 (plate 3) are an example of the remarkably progressive work carried out by the textile department prior to the First World War. The simplified forms and vivid colours were derived from Eastern European ethnic textiles and Expressionist painting. Two other silks from 1925 mix schematized butterflies or flowers drawn from the natural world with purely linear shapes (plates 4 and 5). Textile designs by the Wiener Werkstätte were used for furnishing as well as for dress fabrics, as exemplified by a bodice whose radiating discs already anticipate the dynamic compositions of the 1930s (plate 6).

LUXURY AND EXOTICISM: PARIS AND LYONS

In 1909 Paris was introduced to a brilliantly coloured vision of the Orient through the sets and costumes conceived by Leon Bakst for Diaghilev's series of *Ballets Russes* (mainly ballets by nineteenth-century romantic composers). This was during an era in which pastels and soft shades were favoured sartorial hues. The *Ballets Russes* had performed in Vienna six years previously and its vibrant exoticism obviously struck a chord with the artist-designers of the Wiener Werkstätte's textile department. Poiret, the French couturier, visited Vienna in 1911 and purchased several Wiener Werkstätte fabrics to make up into new fashion creations. He was impressed by Austrian investment in the applied arts and, hoping to achieve similar success, he engaged a number of untutored, working-class girls to design fabric for him. Poiret favoured a spontaneous approach: he would take his students to the zoo, botanical gardens or museums and afterwards ask them to draw and paint their impressions of these locales from memory in a 'naïve' style. The bright, bold, fresh appeal he was aiming for is very apparent in three printed silks from 1919 (plates 7 to 9).

Poiret's Atelier Martine fabrics, like those of the Wiener Werkstätte, were made into household objects such as cushions and curtains as well as fashionable clothing. Raoul Dufy produced textiles for Poiret in a similar vein. He had trained as an artist alongside contemporaries such as the Cubist Braque and had exhibited with the Fauves. Dufy illustrated a book of poems for Apollinaire using woodblock prints and employed the same technique to make textile prints.

The Lyons silk manufacturers Bianchini-Férier attempted in vain to replicate Dufy's best-selling designs but eventually succeeded in persuading him to quit Poiret in 1912. Dufy signed a contract with the firm lasting until 1930, at which date he returned to his first vocation of painting. French Art Deco textiles of the 1920s characteristically imitate an eighteenth-century ideal of opulence, much as Poiret's dresses made reference to the neo-classicism of the French Empire. One example is *Les Toiles de Tournon*, Dufy's series of monochrome or bichromatic block prints on linen. The name as well as the format is reminiscent of the *Toiles de Jouy* produced in France during the eighteenth century to depict narrative scenes interspersed with oversized foliage, in imitation of indigenous Indian prints. *La Chasse* (plate 10) is a black-on-white pastiche of such prints, carried out in a simplified style. *La Danse* (plate 11) depicts a more directly exotic theme.

Based in the Lyons area since the seventeenth century, the silk-weaving industry had always been an important contributor to the French economy in terms of production and exports. The designers and retailers of the luxury fabrics manufactured in the south were usually based in Paris. By the early twentieth century many of the 600 mills in and around Lyons were highly mechanized and produced a variety of woven goods. After World War I there was a shortage of trained weavers, yet an increased demand for silk and supple woven materials including chiffon and lamés. Bianchini-Férier cultivated a good business relationship with the fashionable Parisian designers, bringing prosperity to the area up until the slump of the 1930s.

Dufy became a prolific creator of silks in contrasting colours such as the rose pink and lavender of *Longchamp* (plate 16), showing a fashionable crowd at the races, and the dark red and emerald green leaping horses of *Pegasus* (plate 17). Several other outstanding textile artists ensured the international renown of Bianchini-Férier silks. Alberto-Fabio Lorenzi depicts modishly clad women alternating with bunches of flowers in urns in *La Promenade en bois* (plate 18). His striking contrast of dark blue on lime green is reversed in Georges Barbier's *Venise, fête de nuit* (plate 19), whose radiant patches against a dark background represent the lights of gondolas crossing the lagoon.

Some of the most common icons adapted from eighteenth-century decoration are baskets or urns of flowers and fruit. Flowers also feature in the form of garlands, swags or rosettes. Elements of the pattern are frequently framed by medallions, ovals or octagons. Fountains, trellises, arches, scrolls and spirals are other hallmarks of this revival. Art Deco designers typically recast these devices in a contemporary mould by simplifying and flattening them into unmistakably modern forms. Robert Bonfils employs this technique in *Teheran* (plate 24), a panoply of ellipsoid floral sprays tied with bows. Flora and foliage appear amplified and overpoweringly exotic in *L'Afrique* (plate 25) and *Oasis* (plate 26). The Italian couturier Mariano Fortuny looked back to neo-classicism as well as to the Renaissance for ideas and techniques with which to create unique fabric designs. In one furnishing textile sample lustrous silver vines twist across a dark green silk ground (plate 27).

Carpets were produced to tone in with the lavish interior schemes furnished in these fabrics. Paul Follot, who in 1923 established the interior design firm Pomone, selling goods at Au Bon Marché department store, made carpets to match his furniture, typically decorating the surface with floral arabesques (plate 28). Large blooms proliferate across the expanse of a similar carpet in soft pink and mauve tones comparable to Follot's (plate 29).

This initial decorative style connoted luxury via the symbol of the stylized flower, prominent both in furnishings and dress fabrics of the period. Séguy and Bénédictus illustrated albums of designs for textiles using the 'pochoir' process, an elaborate stencil method, without discriminating between upholstery and clothing (plates 30 and 31). The geometric rose as employed ornamentally by Mackintosh is a favourite motif, appearing in black-and-white on the blue ground of upholstery by Follot (plate 32), in black velvet on a pale chiffon evening scarf (plate 33), and on a blue silk ribbon (plate 34). The mid-1920s' vogue for silver explodes spectacularly into flower from the centre of a shawl by Michel Dubost for Atelier Ducharne (plate 35). Dazzling metallic accessories, such as a second shawl with its gilt border and gold metal thread (plate 36), were a popular choice. A paler dress fabric by Rodier features white flower heads on a cream ground intermingled with chevrons and fan shapes (plate 37).

As textile designers experimented with abstract, two-dimensional elements borrowed from Cubism, they gradually moved away from the lavish decorative surfaces of the early 1920s. Sonia Delaunay, a Russian *émigré* married to the Cubist painter Robert Delaunay, was in the vanguard of this minimalizing aesthetic. During the Paris exhibition of 1925 she showed dresses and fabrics printed with her 'simultaneous' patterns. These were geometric designs based on theories about the interaction of different pigments. The colours, often primaries, were grouped in blocks, stripes or waves for maximum rhythmic impact (plate 38). Delaunay's clear-cut contours are imitated in a silk scarf of the period (plate 39).

The composition of Madame de Andrada's printed furnishing fabric (plate 40) is clearly indebted to abstract painting, combining gradated triangular zones with chequered areas. Pierre Chareau's shading of geometric facets imitates brushstrokes while adopting the more muted Cubist palette (plate 41). His free-flowing doodles, as seen in plate 42, are more reminiscent of Surrealist sketches, however.

1930S MODERNISM

After the financial crisis of 1929, few individuals could afford designer furnishings. The demand for contemporary interior decoration was sustained by commissions from large companies for ocean liners such as the French *Normandie* and the British *Queen Mary*, and for civic buildings such as Claridge's hotel in London and the Odeon cinema chain. Industrial designers were obliged to explore ways of mass-producing cheaper and more durable goods for the general public. The introduction of metal furniture coincided with a move towards a more austere style of interior design. The trend for bright colour had by now given way to a naturalistic range of tones, including pale blue and pink, green, cream, beige, browns, greys and black-and-white. Decoration was no longer overt but was increasingly found in subtle details such as the weave of the fabric.

Textile designers like Bonfils were able to produce schemes in tune with the demand for formalized, linear compositions which became apparent from the late 1920s. *Variations* (plate 46) draws on a type of imagery that developed out of a fascination with new technology, which permitted hitherto unknown speed and mass mechanization. This type of representation was akin to pictorial exploration by the Italian Futurists who had been interested in portraying the accelerated movement of cars, aircraft and machine parts.

Some of the earlier modernistic furnishing textiles still take diagrammatic flowers and leaves as motifs. The roses of *Flower Garden* (plate 47) are discernible as such, although *Flower* (plate 48) is composed of purely angular shapes. An upholstery fabric (plate 49) is almost identical to a Suë et Mare tapestry entitled *Sous Bois* that was shown at the Paris exhibition in 1925. *Quayside* (plate 50) is a scene set at the docks and plate 51 is apparently based on stormy skies. A carpet conceived by Victor Boberman for the Maison de Décoration Intérieure Moderne (DIM) delineates the bodies of acrobats in motion (plate 52).

Other patterns are entirely schematic, repeating figures that may evoke a bird in flight or could equally be based on machine components (plate 53). *Mosaic* (plate 54) is a collage of spotted fragments, and *Prisms* (plate 55) a jigsaw puzzle of triangles. A woven fabric by Rodier (plate 56) contrasts matte and shimmering surfaces forming chevrons, and *Modern Slubb* (plate 57) concentrates attention on the qualities of the combination weave of cotton and artificial silk in the same way.

THE MODERNE: ART DECO IN AMERICA

American interiors in the early 1920s tended to be furnished in a variety of historical revival styles, as there was no dominant contemporary look. Yet US architects led the world in constructing towering office buildings. The interiors of these skyscrapers were decorated in accordance with French taste – the same was true of exterior detailing. The work of French *artistes-décorateurs* became known in 1926 when exhibits from the 1925 Paris exhibition toured the US. Simultaneously, American department stores such as Macy's and Lord and Taylor's began to display and sell French manufactured textiles. Unfortunately, some of the less reputable stores made unauthorized replicas of the best-selling examples, which angered the French.

American designers, hitherto hampered by the reactionary aesthetic choices of their compatriots, were eager to develop in their own direction, however. The Stehli Silks Corporation was one leading manufacturer willing to sponsor innovation by commissioning artists to compose prints suitable for dress fabrics.

To make a change from ubiquitous floral patterns, the company supported the creation of swatches of material depicting the contemporary US lifestyle, once again based on the anecdotal format of the eighteenth-century *Toiles de Jouy*.

The artists' series *Americana* created in 1927 comprises idiosyncratic drawings by Dwight Taylor of a looping rollercoaster, entitled *Thrills* (plate 62), and by Ralph Barton of Paris (plate 63), the city whence Art Deco had come and a magnet for American artists during the 1920s. Barton also records the glamorous jazz age by taking inspiration from the novel title *Gentlemen Prefer Blondes* (plate 65), the story of a flapper turned film-star. Helen Wills, meanwhile, plays on the theme of the American flag in *Stars and Stripes* (plate 64). Perhaps the most innovative of all are the designs that take everyday items for their subjects. Examples are C.B. Falls' *Pegs* (plate 66) and *Moth Balls and Sugar Cubes* (plate 67), in which the renowned photographer Edward Steichen records strikingly lit household objects so that they are defamiliarized into abstraction.

Ruth Reeves is one of the best-known American textile designers of the 1930s. She started her career as a fine artist. Her output was prodigious and she worked in a number of different formats, making furnishing fabrics, tablecloths, hangings and carpets. Reeves' subject matter is very often urban life, as in *Manhattan* (plate 69), which encapsulates the highrise cityscape of the financial capital of the world. The Empire State Building, the Brooklyn Bridge and the Statue of Liberty are no less emblematic of contemporary America than the automobiles, factories, trains and biplanes featured, nor the citizens, typing in offices, taking photographs and enjoying the nightlife. *Homage to Emily Dickinson* (plate 70) appears from its vertical repeat to depict life in an apartment block, from which a woman looks out a window on to a garden full of flowers, cats and birds.

A velveteen hanging was also produced as a voile furnishing fabric to screen windows (plate 71). Incorporating an interior with three women, a platter of fish and bowls of fruit, it recalls Picasso's *Les Demoiselles d'Avignon* and similar compositions in its statuesque figures and flattened arrangement. *Essex Hunt* (plate 72) shows a fox hunt in rural surroundings. The meet outside a large house and the open countryside are framed with foliage which, like the juxtaposition of different scenes, is reminiscent of Dufy's *Longchamp* or *La Chasse*. *Play Boy* (plate 73) imitates the Aztec motifs that Reeves investigated further during a trip to Guatemala in 1934.

INTERNATIONAL ART DECO IN BRITAIN

Although Britain took part in the 1925 Paris exhibition, her entry was not deemed to be of a particularly high quality. Little money was invested in innovative design during this period of economic recession, which succeeded one world war and ended with a second. An effort had been made to promote the contemporary applied arts, however, when the Design and Industries Association (DIA) and the British Institute of Industrial Art (BIIA) were founded in 1915 and 1920 respectively. The BIIA arranged several exhibitions featuring printing and textiles, and when it closed down in 1934, it donated its collection of textiles, of which its holdings were chiefly constituted, to the V&A.

Nonetheless, textile manufacturers were obliged to produce patterns they knew would sell during the 1920s, which were primarily chinoiserie inspired or period reproductions to match the Tudor and Regency revival styles prevalent in British domestic and civic interiors. The first evidence of French influence appeared in 1928 when Schoolbred's London department store displayed articles of furniture by the Maison de Décoration Intérieure Moderne, which later opened an English branch. Then in 1929 Waring & Gillow showed interiors designed by Follot and Chermayeff, subsequently establishing a department to sell French furniture.

The international impact of Art Deco is clearly indicated by the fact that the motifs and materials popular in France and America are reproduced in British textiles of the era. British textile design and manufacture had been strongly influenced by the Arts and Crafts tendencies of the second half of the nineteenth century. Thus designers had directed their energies towards a modest and simple style whose ideal, never to be fulfilled, was to provide handcrafted furnishings for all. When the initial European taste for sumptuous surroundings gave way to a spare, linear modernism, this was more rapidly adopted in Britain and a number of designers such as Marion Dorn made their names by working in this idiom. It is notable that, like Marion Dorn, several leading figures of the period working in Europe and America were émigrés.

From the 1920s, certain established companies were able to bring out lines that reflected worldwide trends alongside their better-selling everyday fabrics. Warner & Sons' *Teheran* (plate 74) is an Arabian Nights fantasy glimpsed through a tracery of exotic archways designed by Bertrand Whittaker in 1925 and used in the interior of Claridge's hotel in London. Printed fabrics were cheaper to make than woven ones, therefore these were more commonly used for experimental or limited runs of textiles. One short-lived project to create innovative decorative objects was that of the Omega workshops, founded by Roger Fry in 1913, although their printed fabrics were produced as part of an artistic rather than a business venture. One example is *Margery* (plate 75) which, despite its tame-sounding name, is a precocious application of abstract art to fabric. Duncan Grant and Vanessa Bell did achieve commercial success, however, when they later worked for Allan Walton Textiles, a firm noted for its open-minded approach. *Grapes* (plate 76) was used for the sofas and curtains of a music room commissioned by the Lefevre Gallery in London.

F. Steiner & Co. produced several printed patterns with an Oriental theme in the early 1920s, among them an example in which tropical trees alternate with Arabic architecture, including mosques (plate 77), and another with fantastically hued peacocks whose tail feathers mimic the blossom-laden trees that overhang them (plate 78). The craze for Egyptian artefacts inspired a scheme imitating the wall decorations of Tutankhamun's tomb excavated in 1922 (plate 79).

The Calico Printers' Association was an amalgamation of Northern English calico-printing firms. Among their early 1920s ranges were floral devices obviously borrowed from French sources (plates 80 and 81). Regimented gardens filled with box trees and trellises echo the backdrops of the pochoir stencils that illustrated Poiret's fashion creations and the Italian fashion plates executed using the same method (plates 82, 83 and 84). Similar examples are another garden scene from Joshua Smith Ltd (plate 85) and the Dufyesque *Futurist* (plate 86) christened by the female designer who created it for Franklin & Franklin.

In the 1930s, Calico Printers' Association designers developed a modernistic repertoire emulating continental abstraction, as can be seen from one scheme featuring boldly shaded overlapping quadrilaterals (plate 88) and another of blocks and arcs (plate 89) whose warp-printed cotton gives a slightly blurred impression. An archetypal Art Deco pattern is inspired by aerodynamic US architecture crowned with radiating beams (plate 90). The CPA appears to have sustained a preference for yellows and reds, then somewhat against the grain. A couple of examples attain the stark simplicity of Russian Productivist textiles, such as *Matelot* (plate 91), in which seagulls in flight and the flared trousers of dancing sailors form contrasting triangular sequences, and *Surfers* (plate 92), which follows the athletic manoeuvres of swimmers on lilos.

William Foxton was considered exceptional among British textile manufacturers for his innovative selection of fabrics. He had sufficient vision to employ artists gifted in the field and won a gold medal in Paris in 1925 with exhibits that included a large-scale flower print by Minnie McLeish (plate 93). McLeish's compositions appear to have been influenced by the Wiener Werkstätte (plate 94). She showed a highly developed colour sense, combining bright shades to stunning effect, as seen in a Cubist flower from 1928 (plate 95). Constance Irving also revisits the sources of Art Deco with her minimal roses on a grid-like ground (plate 96). Claude Lovat Fraser was a painter and illustrator. His bold chevrons and blocks allude to Ancient Egyptian wall paintings (plate 97). F. Gregory Brown, a commercial artist who won his own gold medal at Paris in 1925, foreshadows the illusion of motion later associated with Op Art (plate 99; see also plate 58).

The early 1920s' craze for batik was initiated in France by Madame Marguerite Pangon and popularized in Britain with individually made pieces such as a shawl from 1924–6 by Winifred Kennedy Scott (plate 101), a student at Glasgow School of Art. The characteristic lines made by cracks in the wax during the dyeing process were considered a fault in Indonesia, where the craft originated. In the West some practitioners used them to ornamental effect, however, as can be seen from imitation batik prints such as a screen-printed shawl (plate 102) and the background of plate 78.

Alec Walker, son of a mill owner, produced handblock-printed silks for his own textile firm, Cryséde, which he established in Cornwall. Cryséde specialized in dress fabrics based on Walker's bold, expressive paintings which, like Stehli silk patterns, made a change from commonplace small-scale flowery repeats (plate 104).

By the end of the 1920s, upholstery and curtain fabric became plainer and austerity was judged to be good taste. The contrasting textures of woven fabrics were achieved by mixing natural and artificial fibres such as wool or cotton with rayon. Edinburgh Weavers, the experimental branch of Morton Sundour Fabrics Ltd, was in the forefront of avant-garde woven textile manufacture. Compositions include a medley of sunbursts, zigzags and tiered details (plate 106) and a matching scheme incorporating large torch devices joined by terraces and a sun breaking through clouds (plate 107). The firm also commissioned work from Marion Dorn such as a

tessellating pattern of birds on the wing (plate 108). Old Bleach Linen, an Irish company, issued a similarly pioneering series that included *Mandalay*, Felix Gotto's shoals of fish (plate 109), and a pattern of tree branches (plate 110), each relying for their effect on the rhythmic repetition of arcs.

During the 1930s, accessories such as hangings and rugs might be the only locus of colour amidst an otherwise monochrome décor. The large surface area of carpets was often embellished with a highly textured weave or by cutting into the pile to achieve a three-dimensional effect. Marion Dorn's work was commissioned by celebrities such as the interior decorating consultant Syrie Maugham, for whose 'all white' living-room Dorn produced a cream carpet with a fret pattern formed by the contrast of flat and plain weaves. A rug very similar to this carpet (plate 111) was photographed for the *Architectural Review* in 1935 as the centrepiece of a bedroom in Wells Coates's Modernist Embassy Court Flats in Brighton. Dorn was christened 'the architect of floors' by her contemporaries, and her work was also to be found on board the ships *Orcades* and *Orion,* as well as inside Claridge's hotel.

The Wilton Royal Carpet Factory manufactured many artist-designed carpets, including those of Dorn's husband, Edward McKnight Kauffer. He employed brighter colours in the service of abstraction, overlapping rectangles of scarlet, yellow, blue and green (plate 112). For McKnight Kauffer and Ronald Grierson, both influenced by contemporary painting, the rug provided a similarly shaped format to that of the canvas (plate 113) and many of the floor coverings of the period were woven without traditional carpet borders. Betty Joel's stepped rug (plate 114) is similar in appearance but also employs the textural effect of clipping grooves in the pile to outline the edges of the pattern. A rectangular rug by an unknown designer imitates the spiral designs favoured by Ivan da Silva Bruhns, the best-known Parisian carpet designer of the period (plate 116).

Art Deco was an internationally widespread movement which drew on non-Western cultures, and selected past modes and contemporary technology to create its visual impact. Critics have dismissed it as a style obsessed with surface decoration. Yet the shift in perception characterized by abstraction was a crucial one and it was largely the fabrics made in the 1920s and 1930s, affordable by the majority, which translated this into everyday usage.

1. G. Naylor, *Secession in Vienna Art Nouveau 1890–1914*, V&A Publications, 2000.

PLATES

Measurements are approximate and refer to the size of the object.

PLATE 1
Table cover, woven woollen plush. Design with symmetrical elongated shield-shaped panel.
Holland, 1920s.
132 x 117cm
T.118-1980

PLATE 2
Furnishing fabric, printed cotton. Diagonal meanders of bud-like devices on an irregular mesh sub-pattern.
Probably designed by Charles Rennie Mackintosh for William Foxton, London, 1918.
48.3 x 78.7cm
T.85-1979

PLATE 3
Erlenzeisig, dress fabric, printed silk. Abstract tulip shapes on a white ground.
Designed by Josef Hoffman for the Wiener Werkstätte textile department, Austria, 1910-11.
194.5 x 43.5cm
T.20-1986

PLATE 4
Dress fabric, printed silk. Orange and blue butterflies and snails on a dark ground.
Designed by the Wiener Werkstätte textile department, Austria, *c*.1925.
93 x 50cm
T.21-1986

PLATE 5
Dress fabric, printed silk. Flowers, zigzags and swirls on a dark ground.
Designed by the Wiener Werkstätte textile department, Austria, *c*.1925.
87 x 21cm
T.22-1986

PLATE 6
Bodice, printed silk. Boldly coloured disc shapes on a white and yellow ground.
Designed by the Wiener Werkstätte textile department, Austria, 1910–20.
73 x 24cm
T.855-2000

PLATE 7
Dress fabric, block-printed satin. Yellow and blue flowers on a bright pink ground. Brightly coloured printed silks of this kind were often used by Poiret for lining his couture garments.
Designed by Atelier Martine for Paul Poiret, Paris, 1919.
84 x 43cm
T.539-1919
© ADAGP, Paris and DACS, London 2002

PLATE 8
Dress fabric, block-printed satin. Blue, red and pink flowers on a dark blue ground.
Designed by Atelier Martine for Paul Poiret, Paris, 1919.
84 x 40.5cm
T.540-1919
© ADAGP, Paris and DACS, London 2002

PLATE 9
Dress fabric, block-printed satin. Yellow, purple and pink flowers on a blue ground.
Designed by Atelier Martine for Paul Poiret, Paris, 1919.
84 x 42cm
T.541-1919
© ADAGP, Paris and DACS, London 2002

PLATE 10
La Chasse, furnishing fabric, woodblock-printed linen and cotton. The repeat of a huntsman accompanied by his dog is reversed in alternate rows.
Designed by Raoul Dufy for Bianchini-Férier, Lyons, *c*.1920.
119 x 49.5cm
MISC.2:31-1934
© ADAGP, Paris and DACS, London 2002

PLATE 11
La Danse, furnishing fabric, woodblock-printed cretonne. A sailor
and gypsy dance to the music of an accordion player, surrounded
by large-leafed foliage.
Designed by Raoul Dufy for Bianchini-Férier, Lyons, *c.*1920.
127 x 183cm
CIRC.113-1939
© ADAGP, Paris and DACS, London 2002

PLATE 12
Furnishing fabric, woodblock-printed linen. Large red and
white flowers.
Designed by Raoul Dufy for Bianchini-Férier, Lyons, *c.*1920.
118 x 116.5 cm
MISC.2:29-1934
© ADAGP, Paris and DACS, London 2002

PLATE 13
Grands Feuillages, furnishing fabric, woodblock-printed linen.
Large red and blue leaves.
Designed by Raoul Dufy for Bianchini-Férier, Lyons, *c.*1920.
120 x 126.5cm
MISC.2:30-1934
© ADAGP, Paris and DACS, London 2002

PLATE 14
Les Cornets, furnishing fabric, woodblock-printed linen and cotton.
White arum lilies and five-petalled flowers on a black ground.
Designed by Raoul Dufy for Bianchini-Férier, Lyons, *c.*1924.
101 x 59.5cm
T.9-1932
© ADAGP, Paris and DACS, London 2002

PLATE 15
Les Conques, furnishing fabric, woodblock-printed linen.
Black shells on a white ground.
Designed by Raoul Dufy for Bianchini-Férier, Lyons, 1925.
183 x 122cm
CIRC.112-1939
© ADAGP, Paris and DACS, London 2002

PLATE 16
Longchamp, furnishing fabric, silk. Scenes from the famous
horse-racing course.
Designed by Raoul Dufy for Bianchini-Férier, Lyons, *c.*1931.
96.5 x 64.5cm
T.2-1932
© ADAGP, Paris and DACS, London 2002

PLATE 17
Pegasus, furnishing fabric, silk. Leaping horses alternating with
orchid-like flowers.
Designed by Raoul Dufy for Bianchini-Férier, Lyons, *c.*1931.
96.5 x 63.5cm
T.1-1932
© ADAGP, Paris and DACS, London 2002

PLATE 18
La Promenade en bois, furnishing fabric, silk and mercerized cotton.
Fashionably clad women surrounded by flowers in urns and dogs
chasing each other.
Designed by Alberto-Fabio Lorenzi for Bianchini-Férier, Lyons,
1920s.
96.5 x 64cm
T.4-1932

PLATE 19
Venise, fête de nuit, sample 15292, silk. Gondolas on a lagoon.
Design by Georges Barbier in Bianchini-Férier sample book, 1920.
24 x 22cm
T.219-1992

PLATE 20
En Vacances, sample 15291, silk. Child skipping in a garden, detail
of a larger repeat.
Design by Alberto-Fabio Lorenzi in Bianchini-Férier sample book,
1920.
24 x 17.5cm
T.219-1992

PLATE 21
Sample 15240, silk. Biplane in black and brown.
Bianchini-Férier sample book, 1920.
17 x 14cm
T.219-1992

PLATE 22
Sample 15846, silk. Numbers in black and red.
Bianchini-Férier sample book, 1919.
22 x 9cm
T.220-1992

PLATE 23
Sample 15888, silk. Brilliant flowers on a black background.
Bianchini-Férier sample book, 1919.
25 x 20cm
T.220-1992

PLATE 24
Teheran, furnishing fabric, silk. Repeat of bouquets of flowers.
Designed by Robert Bonfils for Bianchini-Férier, Lyons, 1925–8.
140 x 95cm
MISC.2:36-1934

PLATE 25
L'Afrique, furnishing fabric, silk. Yellow and gold flowers with blue leaves.
Designed by Robert Bonfils for Bianchini-Férier, Lyons, 1925–8.
94.5 x 65cm
CIRC.170-1932

PLATE 26
Oasis, furnishing fabric, silk. Sheaves of exotic leaves.
Designed by Robert Bonfils for Bianchini-Férier, Lyons, 1925–9.
131 x 142.5cm
MISC.2:28-1934

PLATE 27
Furnishing fabric sample, embossed linen. Silver vines on a drab green ground.
Designed by Mariano Fortuny, Italy, 1927.
34 x 28cm
CIRC.807-1967

PLATE 28
Carpet, hand-knotted wool. Pink ground with a surface pattern of black, branching spirals and pink and yellow flowers.
Designed by Paul Follot, Paris, 1919–20.
200 x 150cm
T.77-1982

PLATE 29
Carpet, hand-knotted wool. Busy, large-scale floral design in pinks and mauves with contrasting neutrals.
Probably French, 1923–7.
304.5 x 152cm
T.393-1977

PLATE 30
Bookplate 20 from *Papillons: vingt planches en phototypie coloriées au patron donnant 81 papillons et 16 compositions décoratives*.
By E.A. Séguy, published by Tolmer, Paris, 1920s.
49.D.13

PLATE 31
Bookplate 20 from *Variations: quatre-vingt-six motifs décoratifs en vingt planches*.
By Edouard Bénédictus, published by A. Lévy, Paris, 1924.
49.E.21

PLATE 32
Armchair by Groult upholstered in silk fabric. Black-and-white roses and stripes of small black leaves on a blue ground.
Fabric designed by Paul Follot, Paris, 1920.
Height 103.5 x width 82cm
W.45-1981

PLATE 33
Scarf. Clusters of black cut velvet roses on a pale grey chiffon ground.
Probably made in Lyons, c.1920.
152.5 x 54.5cm
T.267-1972

PLATE 34
Ribbon, silk. Blue ground with a design of roses and leaves woven in black.
France, 1920s–30s.
35.5 x 6.5cm
T.268-1967

PLATE 35
Panel, probably intended for a shawl. Pale grey silk crêpe with a
large central stylized floral and foliate arrangement woven in
silver gilt.
Michel Dubost for Atelier Ducharne, Paris, c.1925.
137 x 114cm
T.321-1979

PLATE 36
Shawl, woven and printed. Square with a deep border. Black
chiffon decorated with gilt threads and printed with rows of small
squares shading from mid-blue to cream.
Lyons, c.1925.
117 x 117cm
T.248-1981

PLATE 37
Dress fabric made into a shawl. Cream silk crêpe machine-
embroidered in cream silk floss with vertical chevron bands, ray
devices and flower heads.
Manufactured by Rodier, France, c.1928.
135 x 108cm
T.831-1974

PLATE 38
Screen-printed silk organza. Black and primary-coloured blocks.
Produced by Ascher Ltd, London, 1967, from an original design by
Sonia Delaunay, 1925–7.
99.5 x 106cm
CIRC.1091-1967

PLATE 39
Scarf, printed silk. Purple, grey and white linear design.
Probably French, 1925.
193 x 97cm
T.266-1972

PLATE 40
Furnishing fabric, seven-coloured screen- or block- and resist-
printed cotton. A photograph of the design appears in the catalogue
of the 1925 Paris exhibition in the section on French wallpaper
(Plate LXXXIII). The paper was designed by Madame de Andrada
and manufactured by Paul Dumas.
Designed by Madame de Andrada, France, 1925.
468 x 72.5cm
T.88-1973

PLATE 41
Furnishing fabric, block-printed linen. Shaded abstract shapes.
Designed by Pierre Chareau, France, 1927–8.
100 x 129.5cm
MISC.2:34-1934

PLATE 42
Furnishing fabric, block-printed linen. Surrealist doodles.
Designed by Pierre Chareau, France, 1920s.
98 x 128.5cm
MISC.2:35-1934

PLATE 43
Upholstery sample, cotton plush. Repeat of blocks and circles with
decorative infills on a voided orange ground.
Probably French, 1925–30.
132 x 117cm
T.120-1980

PLATE 44
Furnishing fabric, cotton plush. Geometric shapes in yellow with
contrasting subdued tones.
French, c.1925.
129 x 107cm
T.121-1980

PLATE 45
Furnishing fabric, cotton plush. Interlinked quadrilaterals with
stippled areas.
French, c.1925.
132 x 107cm
T.122-1980

PLATE 46
Variations, furnishing fabric, silk. Concentric circles and zigzags, blue on white.
Designed by Robert Bonfils for Bianchini-Férier, Lyons, c.1931.
119 x 96.5cm
T.6-1932

PLATE 47
Flower Garden, furnishing fabric, cotton and artificial silk. Pink rose heads woven in a raised pattern on a ground of pink and blue.
France, 1931.
91.5 x 61cm
CIRC.753-1931

PLATE 48
Flower, furnishing fabric, cotton and artificial silk. Angular forms in light blue and pink on a diapered ground.
France, 1931.
91.5 x 63.5cm
T.219-1931

PLATE 49
Furnishing fabric, woven. Grey and green cotton damask with a grey silk weft. The composition of overlapping leaves is worked in alternating paler and darker silks and is very similar to the velvet tapestry *Sous Bois* shown by Süe and Mare in the 1925 Paris exhibition (Catalogue Plate XXXVI).
Made in France for Betty Joel Ltd, 1928.
132 x 205.5cm
CIRC.31A-1936

PLATE 50
Quayside, furnishing fabric, artificial silk. Urban waterside scene in brown and pale blue on a cream ground.
France, c.1931.
91.5 x 63.5cm
T.217-1931

PLATE 51
Furnishing fabric, woven. Grey cotton damask with a weft of blue, green and yellow silks. Depicts stylized clouds, stormy weather and rough seas.
Made in France for Betty Joel Ltd, c.1930.
132 x 31cm
CIRC.26-1936

PLATE 52
Carpet, hand-knotted wool. Dark brown ground with a linear depiction of three acrobats in action, outlined in red and cream. Signed 'DIM' in cream in the pile.
Victor Boberman for Maison de Décoration Intérieure Moderne (DIM), Paris, 1928–9.
300 x 194.5cm
T.366-1977

PLATE 53
Furnishing fabric, damask and silk. Dynamic abstract shapes in grey and orange on a buff-coloured ground.
Made in France for Betty Joel Ltd, c.1930.
132 x 60.5cm
CIRC.24-1936

PLATE 54
Mosaic, furnishing fabric, cotton and artificial silk. Overlapping triangular forms spotted with yellow and red.
France, 1931.
91.5 x 66cm
T.220-1931

PLATE 55
Prisms, furnishing fabric, cotton and artificial silk. A kaleidoscope of geometric forms in pale blue and ochre, much of the pattern deriving from the textures of different weaves.
France, c.1931.
91.5 x 63.5cm
T.214-1931

PLATE 56
Furnishing fabric, silk. Grey and white with chevron motifs.
Manufactured by Rodier, France, 1920s.
126 x 106.5cm
MISC.2:37-1934

PLATE 57
Modern Slubb, furnishing fabric, cotton and artificial silk. Rows of checked zigzags and horizontally striped triangles.
France, 1931.
66 x 45.5cm
CIRC.752-1931

PLATE 58
Part of a wool and cotton hanging. A repeating sequence of black, grey and white undulating lines.
Designed by Jean Bouzois for Metz and Co., Holland, c.1930.
71 x 63cm
CIRC.46-1936

PLATE 59
Dress fabric, lightweight wool and silk. Printed with a bold pattern of overlapping planes of magenta, beige and blue outlined in black.
Designed for Chanel, France, 1929.
65 x 48cm
T.191-1975

PLATE 60
Part of a hanging, printed cotton. This fabric was exhibited at and received from the Exhibition of Austrian Art, Dorland Hall, Lower Regent Street, held in May 1934.
Designed by Grete Zwiesele of the Gewerkförderungsinstitut in Bregenz, Austria, 1934.
63 x 51 cm
CIRC.102D-1934

PLATE 61
Araby, furnishing fabric, cotton and artificial silk. Cubes, circles and cloud forms woven in a shiny raised pattern in cream on a pale blue matte ground.
France, c.1931.
91.5 x 61cm
T.215-1931

PLATE 62
Thrills, dress fabric, printed silk crêpe de Chine. Silhouette of switchback in cream on a rust-coloured ground.
Designed by Dwight Taylor for the Stehli Silks Corporation, New York, 1927.
30.5 x 28.5cm
T.87G-1930

PLATE 63
Map of Paris, dress fabric, printed silk crêpe de Chine. Bird's-eye view of Paris. Similar to *Plan de Paris*, a dress fabric designed by Pierre Dumas of Ateliers A.G.B. and featured in the 1925 Paris exhibition (Catalogue, Plate XXVIII).
Designed by Ralph Barton for the Stehli Silks Corporation, New York, 1927.
58.5 x 49.5cm
T.87I-1930

PLATE 64
Stars and Stripes, dress fabric, printed silk crêpe de Chine. Red and white stars in loops on a navy ground.
Designed by Helen Wills for the Stehli Silks Corporation, New York, 1927.
32.5 x 30cm
T.87E-1930

PLATE 65
Gentlemen Prefer Blondes, dress fabric, printed silk crêpe de Chine. Men in top hats focusing their attention on blonde women.
Designed by Ralph Barton for the Stehli Silks Corporation, New York, 1927.
50 x 47.5cm
T.87L-1930

PLATE 66
Pegs, dress fabric, printed silk crêpe de Chine. Three-dimensional pegs on a scarlet ground.
Designed by C.B. Falls for the Stehli Silks Corporation, New York, 1927.
22.5 x 20.5cm
T.87M-1930

PLATE 67
Moth Balls and Sugar Cubes, dress fabric, printed silk crêpe de Chine. Design adapted from a photograph of moth balls and sugar cubes lit from different angles.
Designed by Edward Steichen for the Stehli Silks Corporation, New York, 1927.
20.5 x 19cm
T.87P-1930

PLATE 68
Dress fabric, printed silk crêpe de Chine. Brightly coloured apples, pears, cherries and grapes against a dark ground.
Manufactured by the Stehli Silks Corporation, New York, 1930.
49 x 49cm
T.88C-1930

PLATE 69
Manhattan, hanging, printed cotton. New York City in the 1930s.
Designed by Ruth Reeves for W. & J. Sloane, New York, 1930.
254 x 94cm
T.57-1932

PLATE 70
Homage to Emily Dickinson, furnishing fabric, printed cotton velvet. Repeat of woman looking from an apartment window into a garden.
Designed by Ruth Reeves for W. & J. Sloane, New York, 1930.
266 x 137cm
CIRC.282A-1932

PLATE 71
Hanging, printed cotton voile. Cubist-inspired female figures in an interior with dishes of food.
Designed by Ruth Reeves for W. & J. Sloane, New York, 1930.
220 x 117cm
T.56-1932

PLATE 72
Essex Hunt, furnishing fabric, printed cotton. Hunt scenes framed by foliage.
Designed by Ruth Reeves for W. & J. Sloane, New York, 1930.
274 x 104cm
T.58-1932

PLATE 73
Play Boy, printed cotton and monk's cloth. Figures shooting, riding and driving represented in Aztec-style block motifs.
Designed by Ruth Reeves for W. & J. Sloane, New York, 1930.
127 x 71cm
CIRC.276-1932

PLATE 74
Teheran, furnishing fabric, silk, linen and rayon. An exotic landscape is silhouetted in white against a sky of variegated pink and blue weft, seen through arches evoking Islamic architecture. This textile was used in the interior of Claridge's hotel in London.
Designed by Bertrand Whittaker for Warner & Sons, Essex, 1925.
92.5 x 63.5cm
T.200-1972

PLATE 75
Margery, furnishing fabric, linen printed with wood and metal blocks. Cone shapes filled in with brushstrokes.
Designed by Omega Workshops, London and printed at the Maromme printworks in Rouen, 1913.
76 x 54.5cm
T.386B-1913

PLATE 76
Grapes, furnishing fabric, printed linen. Grey and white vines, leaves and flowers on a bright yellow ground. Used as upholstery and drapery for a music room on display in the Lefevre Gallery showroom, London.
Designed by Duncan Grant for Allan Walton Textiles, London, 1932.
156 x 127cm
CIRC.236B-1935
© Duncan Grant Estate, 1978. Courtesy of Henrietta Garnett

PLATE 77
Furnishing fabric, roller-printed cotton. Middle-Eastern-style buildings alternate with tropical trees.
Manufactured by F. Steiner & Co., Lancashire, 1923.
76 x 54.5cm
CIRC.467-1966

PLATE 78
Furnishing fabric, roller-printed cotton. Peacocks and blossom trees on a bronze ground veined with white.
Manufactured by F. Steiner & Co., Lancashire, 1922.
94 x 91.5cm
CIRC.454-1966

PLATE 79
Furnishing fabric, roller-printed cotton. Imitation Egyptian wall paintings and hieroglyphics.
Manufactured by F. Steiner & Co., Lancashire, 1920s.
77 x 76cm
CIRC.668-1966

PLATE 80
Furnishing fabric, roller-printed cotton. Stylized roses in pale colours against a dark ground.
Manufactured by the Calico Printers' Association, Manchester, 1919.
68 x 46cm
CIRC.613-1964

PLATE 81
Furnishing fabric, roller-printed cotton. Stylized flower heads in pale colours against a dark blue and purple ground.
Manufactured by the Calico Printers' Association, Manchester, 1920.
91.5 x 33cm
CIRC.441-1966

PLATE 82
Furnishing fabric, roller-printed cotton. Pattern of box trees and trellises.
Manufactured by the Calico Printers' Association, Manchester, 1921.
91.5 x 89cm
CIRC.447-1966

PLATE 83
Furnishing fabric, roller-printed cotton. Trellis with large bunches of flowers and fruits.
Manufactured by F.W. Grafton & Co., Manchester, 1921.
112 x 86.5cm
T.442-1934

PLATE 84
Dress fabric, roller-printed cotton. A couple dressed in eighteenth-century court costume with pink dogs and flowers on a dark ground.
Designed by George Sheringham for Tootal Broadhurst Lee & Co., Manchester, 1925.
124.5 x 91.5cm
CIRC.475-1966

PLATE 85
Furnishing fabric, roller-printed cotton satin. Trees in boxes and pots with garden vistas through trellised arches and balustrades.
Manufactured by Joshua Smith Ltd, Britain, 1923.
75 x 47cm
CIRC.618-1964

PLATE 86
Futurist, furnishing fabric, roller-printed cotton. Black-and-white blooms superimposed on brightly coloured vertical stripes.
Manufactured by Franklin & Franklin, Britain, 1920.
76 x 51cm
T.16-1939

PLATE 87
Furnishing fabric, roller-printed cotton. Flowers intercut with leaf blades.
Manufactured by the Calico Printers' Association, Manchester, 1927.
80 x 80cm
CIRC.491-1966

PLATE 88
Furnishing fabric, roller-printed cotton. Diamonds striped in bright colours.
Manufactured by the Calico Printers' Association, Manchester, 1933.
119 x 78.5cm
T.100-1979

PLATE 89
Furnishing fabric, warp-printed cotton. Blocks, arcs and waves in bright, softened colours.
Manufactured by the Calico Printers' Association, Manchester, 1933.
76 x 52cm
T.111-1979

PLATE 90
Furnishing fabric, warp-printed cotton. Cone-shaped radiating motifs.
Manufactured by the Calico Printers' Association, Manchester, 1929.
63.5 x 56cm
T.94-1979

PLATE 91
Matelot, dress fabric, roller-printed cotton. Dancing sailors and flying seagulls.
Manufactured by the Calico Printers' Association, Manchester, 1934.
73.5 x 51.5cm
T.244-1987

PLATE 92
Surfers, dress fabric, roller-printed cotton. Bathers surfing on lilos.
Manufactured by the Calico Printers' Association, Manchester, 1937.
75 x 65cm
T.264-1987

PLATE 93
Furnishing fabric, roller-printed cretonne. Large-scale flowers in a hand-painted style. The motifs show the influence of late seventeenth- and early eighteenth-century English textiles. This textile was shown at the 1925 Paris exhibition.
Designed by Minnie McLeish for William Foxton, London, 1923.
151 x 79cm
T.368-1934

PLATE 94
Furnishing fabric, roller-printed cotton. Bluebell-shaped flowers and organic forms very similar in style, scale and colours to some Wiener Werkstätte textiles.
Designed by Minnie McLeish for William Foxton, London, 1924.
249 x 79cm
T.413-1934

PLATE 95
Furnishing fabric, roller-printed cotton. Boldly coloured Cubist flowers.
Designed by Minnie McLeish for William Foxton, London, 1928.
206 x 79cm
T.400-1934

PLATE 96
Furnishing fabric, roller-printed cretonne. Idiosyncratic blue and grey plaid with simplified pink roses.
Designed by Constance Irving for William Foxton, London, c.1926.
83.5 x 40.5cm
CIRC.630-1956

PLATE 97
Furnishing fabric, roller-printed cretonne. Design based on Egyptian wall paintings.
Designed by Claude Lovat Fraser for William Foxton, London, 1922.
114 x 81cm
T.440-1934

PLATE 98
Furnishing fabric, roller-printed cotton. Abstract shapes, reminiscent of architecture or machinery.
Designed by W. Herrman for William Foxton, London, 1928.
78.5 x 42cm
CIRC.566-1966

PLATE 99
Furnishing fabric, printed linen. This arch pattern in blacks and greys was displayed at the Paris exhibition in 1925.
Designed by F. Gregory Brown for William Foxton, London, 1922.
112 x 94cm
T.325-1934

PLATE 100
Furnishing fabric, roller-printed cotton. Pattern of alternating dark and bright triangles on which small diamonds of a paler hue are superimposed.
Manufactured by Arthur Sanderson & Sons Ltd, Uxbridge, 1928.
76 x 43cm
CIRC.623-1964

PLATE 101
Shawl, batik resist-dyed silk crêpe de Chine. Each corner of the shawl is decorated with blossoming branches among which are perched long-tailed birds.
Made by Winifred Kennedy Scott, Britain, 1924–6.
188 x 180.5cm
T.112-1975

PLATE 102
Shawl, screen-printed silk. The design, in particular the fine network of lines in the background, imitates batik.
Manufactured by Langley Prints, Britain, 1926.
176.5 x 88cm
T.84-1964

PLATE 103
Furnishing fabric, roller-printed cretonne. This textile mimics the compartmentalized areas filled with small-scale decoration found in Indonesian batik designs. The original design is in the Hunterian Art Gallery, Glasgow.
Possibly designed by Charles Rennie Mackintosh for William Foxton, London, 1922.
89 x 78.5cm
T.439-1934

PLATE 104
Cornish Farm, dress fabric, block-printed silk. Painterly pattern of small stylized houses within a garden setting.
Designed by Alec Walker for Crysède Ltd, Cornwall, 1930.
61 x 48cm
T.63-1979

PLATE 105
Disc, furnishing fabric, silk. Large white discs on a pale blue background linked by horizontal bands.
Manufactured by Warner & Sons, Essex, 1924.
130.5 x 68cm
T.203-1972

PLATE 106
Furnishing fabric, linen cotton. A busy, small-scale abstract scheme in dark orange on a buff ground.
Designed by St Edmundsbury Weavers for Edinburgh Weavers, Carlisle, c.1930.
69 x 66.5cm
CIRC.805-1967

PLATE 107
Furnishing fabric, linen cotton. Torch-shaped devices, tiers and sunbursts in dark orange on a buff ground.
Designed by St Edmundsbury Weavers for Edinburgh Weavers, Carlisle, c.1930.
104 x 70.5cm
CIRC.804-1967

PLATE 108
Avis, furnishing fabric, rayon, spun rayon and cotton. Schematic birds in flight.
Designed by Marion Dorn for Edinburgh Weavers, Carlisle, c.1939.
45.5 x 43cm
CIRC.319C-1939

PLATE 109
Mandalay, furnishing fabric, reversible linen. A stylized shoal of fish.
Designed by Felix C. Gotto for Old Bleach Linen, Northern Ireland, c.1935.
160 x 127cm
CIRC.223-1935

PLATE 110
Furnishing fabric, linen and artificial silk. A composition of sinuous tree branches.
Manufactured by Old Bleach Linen, Northern Ireland, c.1936.
64.5 x 63.5cm
CIRC.116-1937

24

PLATE III
Rug, hand-knotted wool. Cream-coloured design of maze-like
interlocking shapes formed by the varying thickness of the pile.
Designed by Marion Dorn, for the the Wilton Royal Carpet Factory
Ltd, near Salisbury, c.1934.
200 x 122cm
CIRC.480-1974

PLATE 112
Rug, hand-knotted woollen pile on a jute warp. Overlapping
multicoloured rectangles and vertical stripes.
Designed by Edward McKnight Kauffer for the Wilton Royal Carpet
Factory, near Salisbury, 1929.
210.5 x 113.5cm
T.440-1971

PLATE 113
Carpet, hand-knotted wool. Abstract design resembling synthetic
cubist works by Braque and Picasso, signed in the pile.
Designed by Ronald Grierson and made in India, 1935.
272 x 189 cm
T.440-1976

PLATE 114
Rug, hand-knotted pile of wool and bast fibres on a cotton warp.
Geometric bands, stripes and a circle.
Made in China for Betty Joel Ltd, 1930s.
180.5 x 105cm
T.296-1977

PLATE 115
Rug, hand-knotted woollen pile on a jute warp. A central design of
overlapping curved forms on a cream ground. Includes the artist's
initials.
Designed by Serge Chermayeff, probably for the Wilton Royal
Carpet Factory Ltd, near Salisbury, 1930.
152.5 x 139.5cm
T.157-1978

PLATE 116
Carpet, hand-knotted wool with a jute and hemp weft. Red and
black rectangular spirals on a cream ground.
Probably made in Britain, 1930s.
145 x 145cm
T.100-1999

PLATE 1. Table cover. T.118-1980

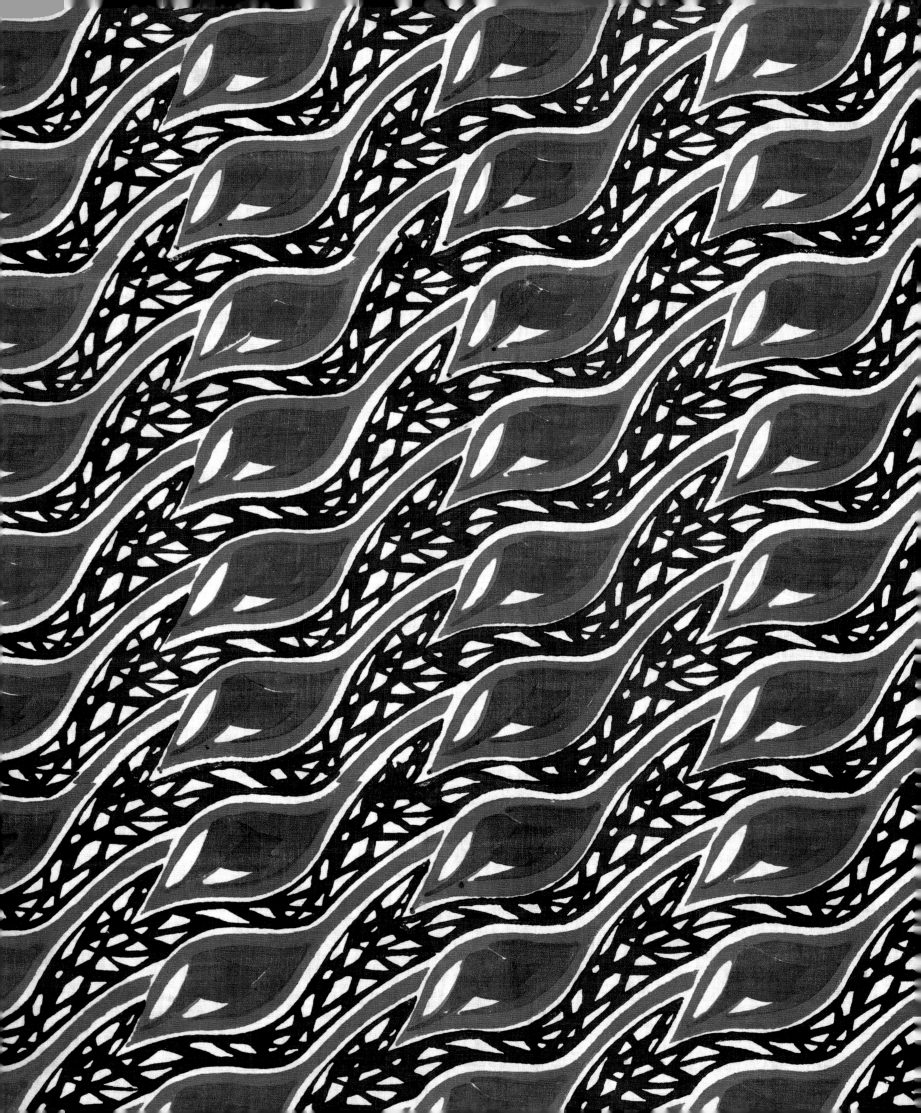

PLATE 2. Furnishing fabric. T.85-1979

PLATE 3. *Erlenzeisig*, dress fabric. T.20-1986

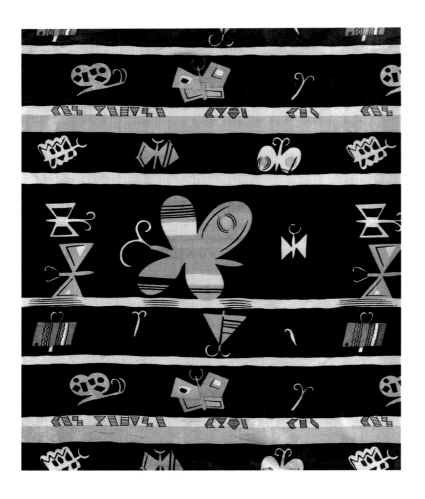

PLATE 4. Dress fabric. T.21-1986

PLATE 5. Dress fabric. T.22-1986

29

PLATE 6. Bodice. T.855-2000

PLATE 7. Dress fabric. T.539-1919

30

PLATE 8. Dress fabric. T.540-1919

PLATE 9. Dress fabric. T.541-1919

PLATE 10. *La Chasse*, furnishing fabric. MISC.2:31-1934

PLATE 11. *La Danse*, furnishing fabric. CIRC.113-1939

PLATE 12. Furnishing fabric. MISC.2:29-1934

34

PLATE 13. *Grands Feuillages*, furnishing fabric. MISC.2:30-1934

PLATE 14. *Les Cornets*, furnishing fabric. T.9-1932

PLATE 15. *Les Conques,* furnishing fabric. CIRC.112-1939

PLATE 16. *Longchamp*, furnishing fabric. T.2-1932   PLATE 17. *Pegasus*, furnishing fabric. T.1-1932

PLATE 18. *La Promenade en Bois*, furnishing fabric. T.4-1932

PLATE 19. *Venise, fête de nuit*, sample 15292. T.219-1992

PLATE 20. *En Vacances*, sample 15291. T.219-1992

Plate 21. Sample 15240. T.219-1992

PLATE 22. Sample 15846. T.220-1992

42

PLATE 23. Sample 15888. T.220-1992

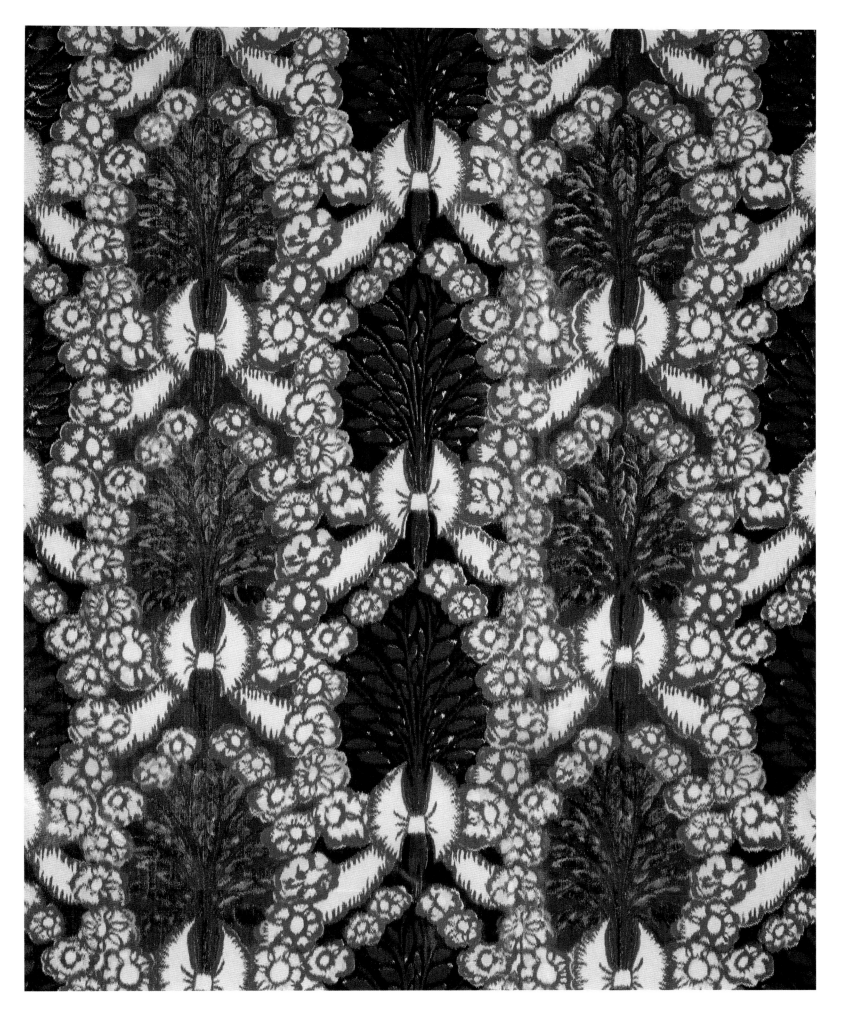

43

PLATE 24. *Teheran*, furnishing fabric. MISC.2:36-1934

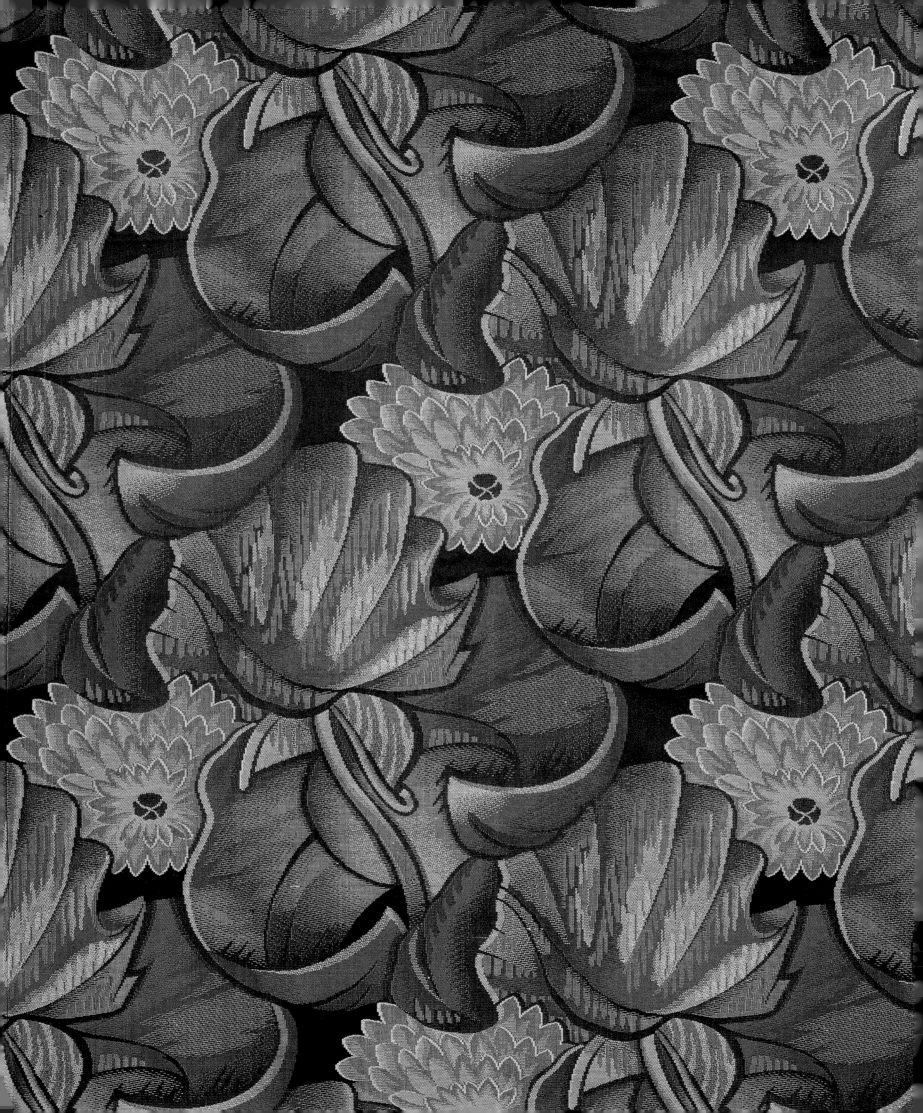

PLATE 25. *L'Afrique*, furnishing fabric. CIRC.170-1932

45

PLATE 26. *Oasis*, furnishing fabric. MISC.2:28-1934

PLATE 27. Furnishing fabric sample. CIRC.807-1967

PLATE 28. Carpet. T.77-1982

PLATE 29. Carpet. T.393-1977

Pl. 20

PLATE 30. Bookplate. 49.D.13

PLATE 31. Bookplate. 49.E.21

PLATE 32. Armchair. W.45:1-1981

52

PLATE 33. Scarf. T.267-1972

PLATE 34. Ribbon. T.268-1967

54

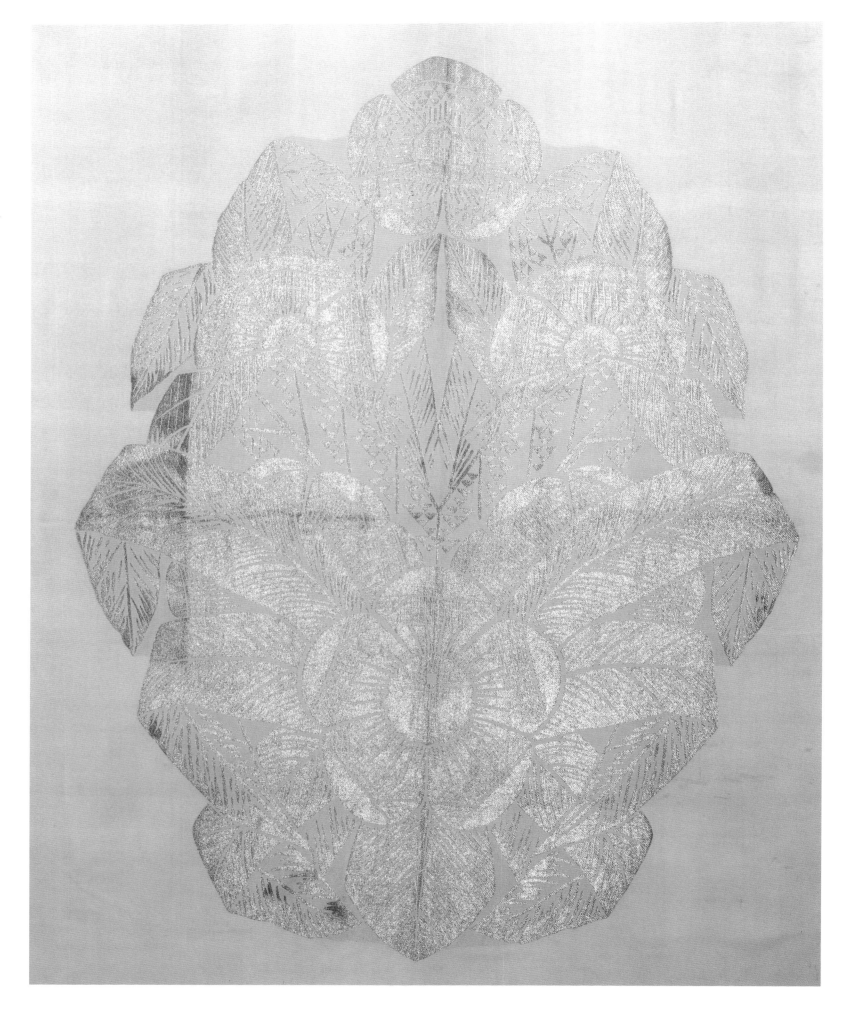

PLATE 35. Panel, probably intended for a shawl. T.321-1979

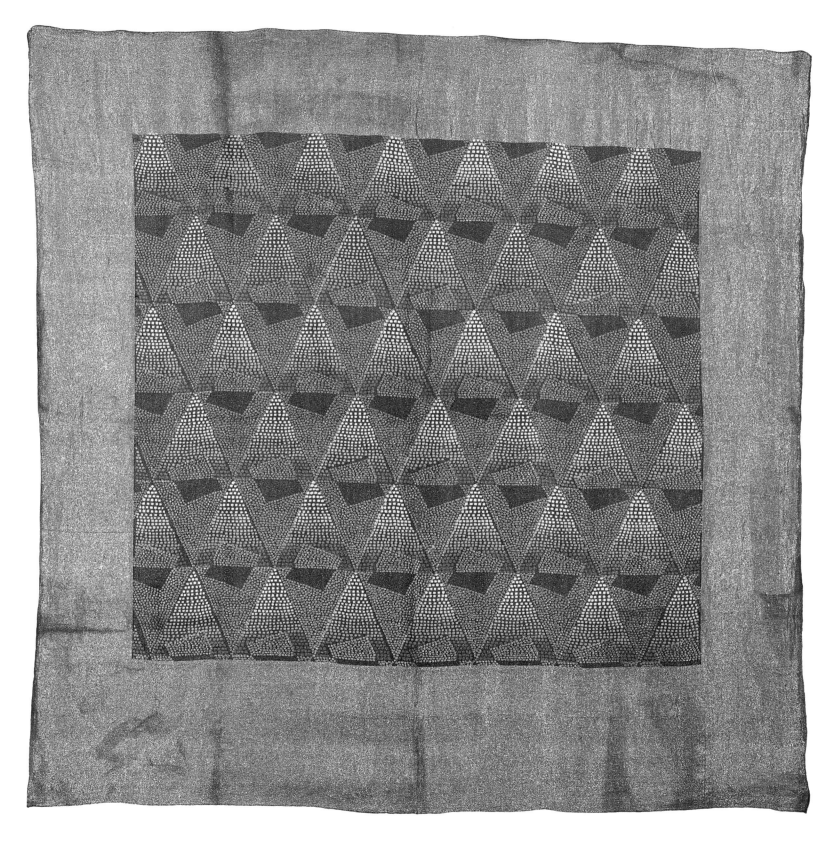

PLATE 36. Shawl. T.248-1981

PLATE 36. Shawl (detail). T.248-1981

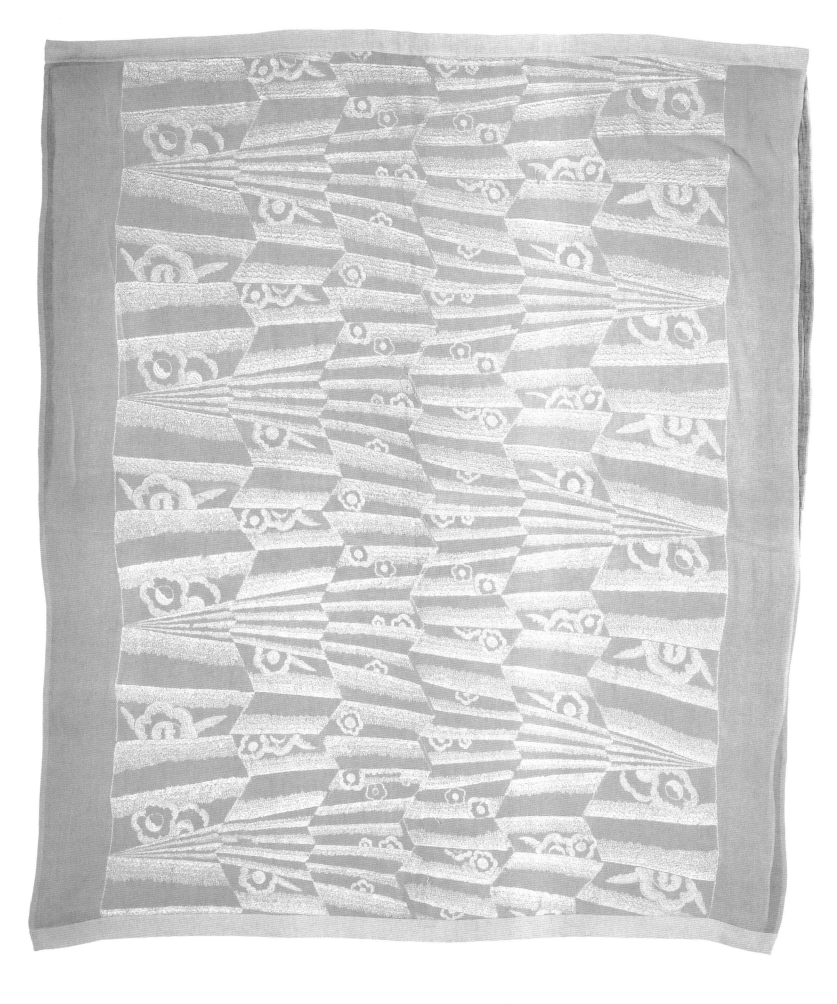

Plate 37. Dress fabric. T.831-1974

PLATE 38. Screen-printed silk organza. CIRC.1091-1967

59

PLATE 39. Scarf. T.266-1972

PLATE 40. Furnishing fabric. T.88-1973

PLATE 41. Furnishing fabric. MISC.2:34-1934

PLATE 42. Furnishing fabric. MISC.2:35-1934

64

PLATE 43. Upholstery sample. T.120-1980

PLATE 44. Furnishing fabric. T.121-1980

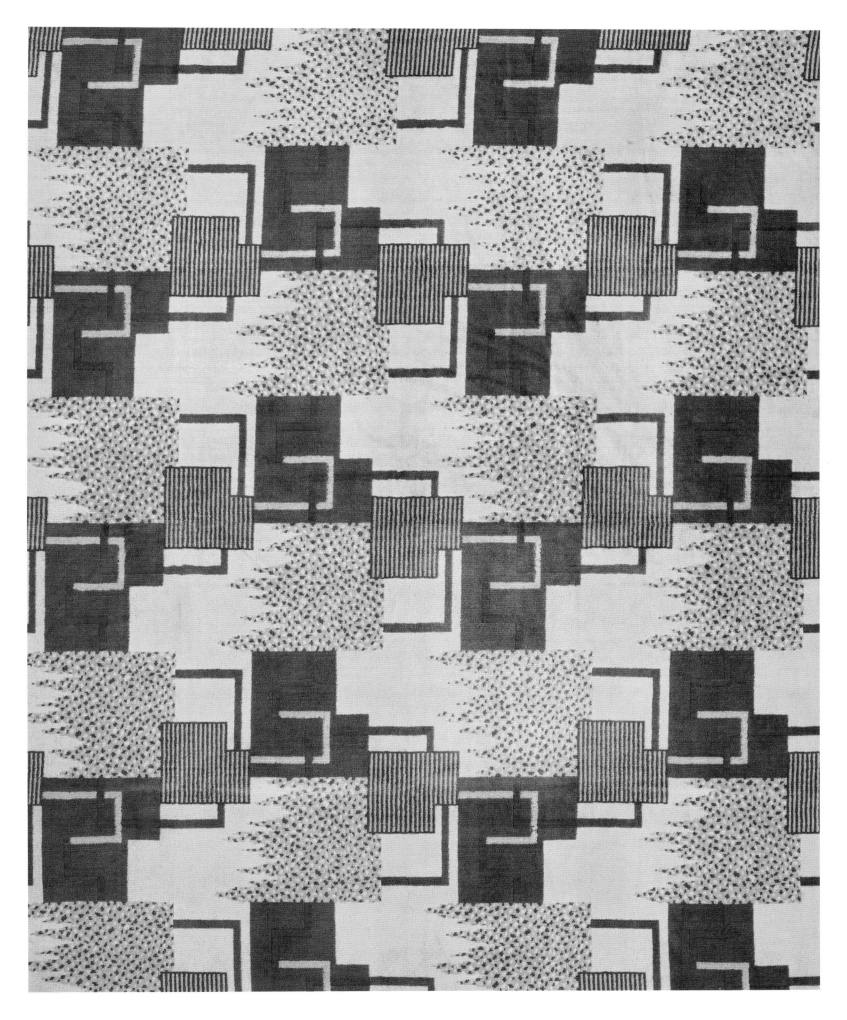

PLATE 45. Furnishing fabric. T.122-1980

PLATE 46. *Variations*, furnishing fabric. T.6-1932

PLATE 47. *Flower Garden*, furnishing fabric. CIRC.753-1931

PLATE 48. *Flower*, furnishing fabric. T.219-1931

68

PLATE 49. Furnishing fabric. CIRC.31A-1936

PLATE 50. *Quayside*, furnishing fabric. T.217-1931

PLATE 51. Furnishing fabric. CIRC.26-1936

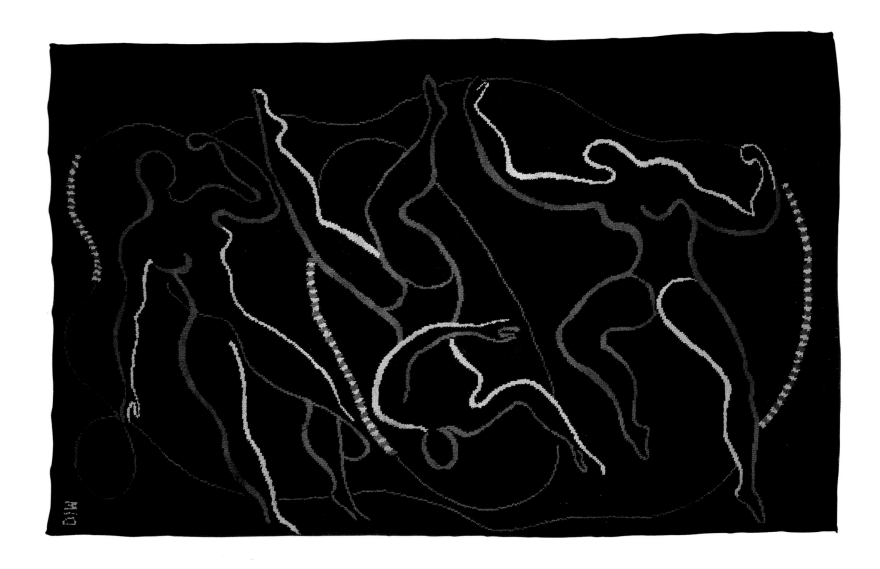

PLATE 52. Carpet. T.366-1977

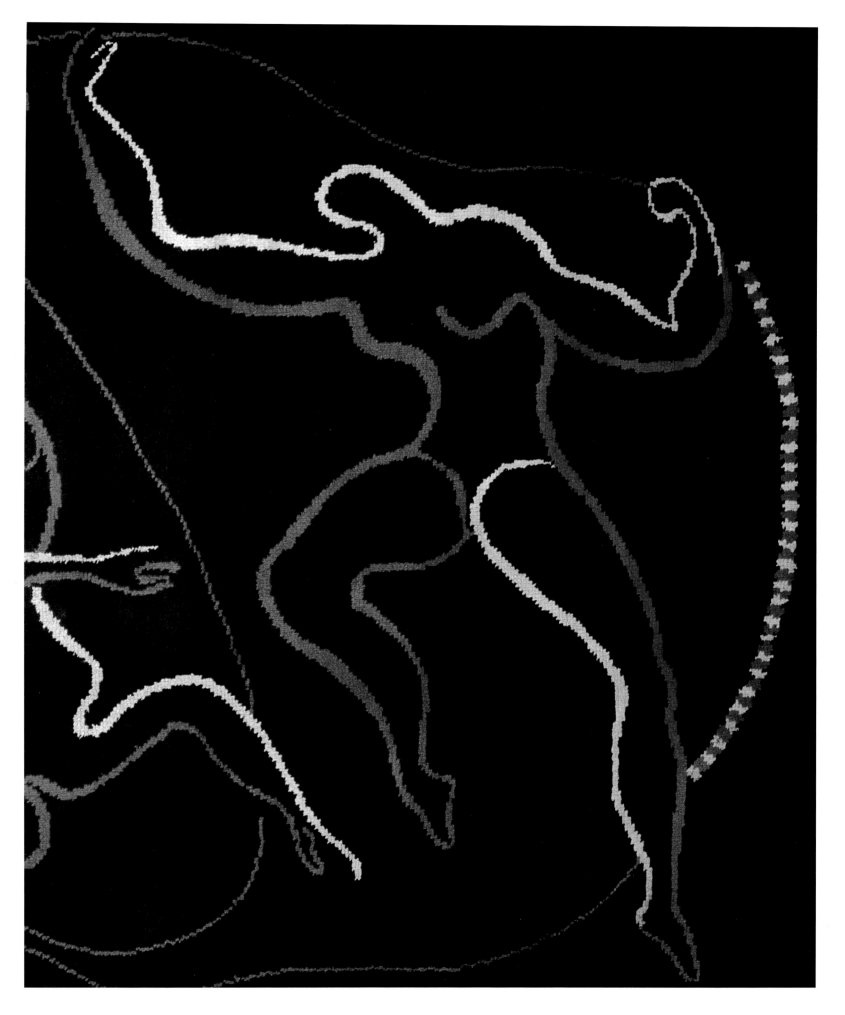

73

PLATE 52. Carpet (detail). T.366-1977

PLATE 55. *Prisms*, furnishing fabric. T.214-1931

PLATE 53. Furnishing fabric. CIRC.24-1936

74

PLATE 53. Furnishing fabric. CIRC.24-1936

PLATE 54. *Mosaic*, furnishing fabric. T.220-1931

PLATE 56. Furnishing fabric. MISC.2:37-1934

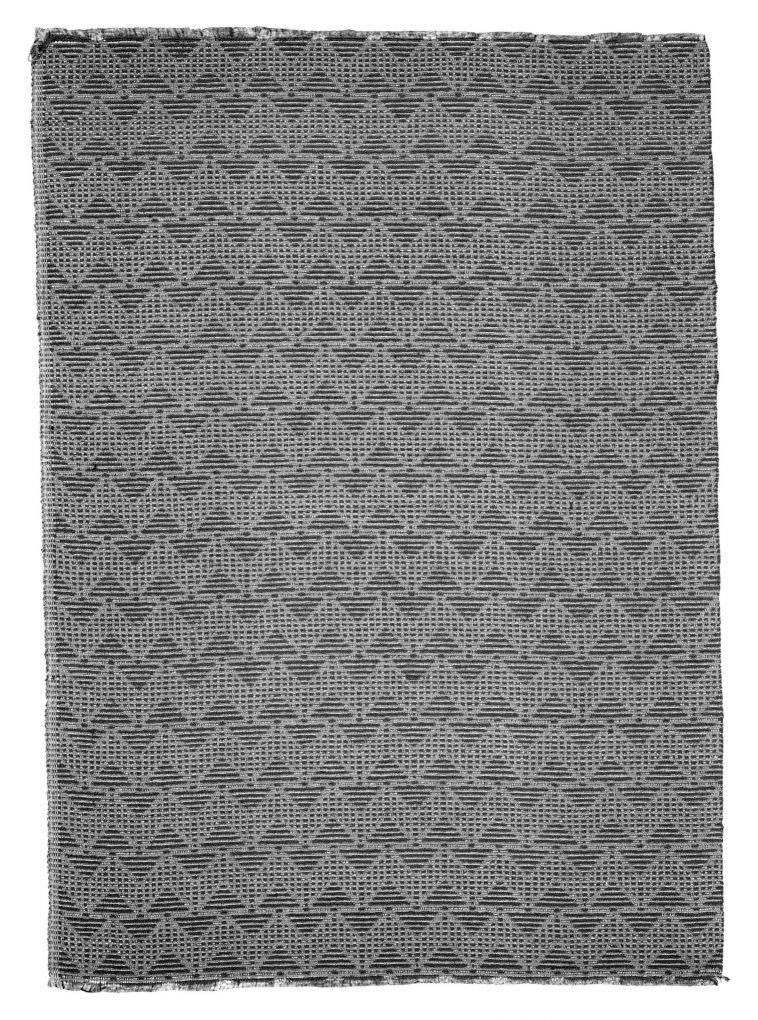

PLATE 57. *Modern Slubb*, furnishing fabric. CIRC.752-1931

PLATE 58. Part of a wool and cotton hanging. CIRC.46-1936

79

PLATE 59. Dress fabric. T.191-1975

PLATE 60. Part of a hanging. CIRC.102D-1934

PLATE 61. *Araby*, furnishing fabric. T.215-1931

PLATE 62. *Thrills*, dress fabric. T.87G-1930

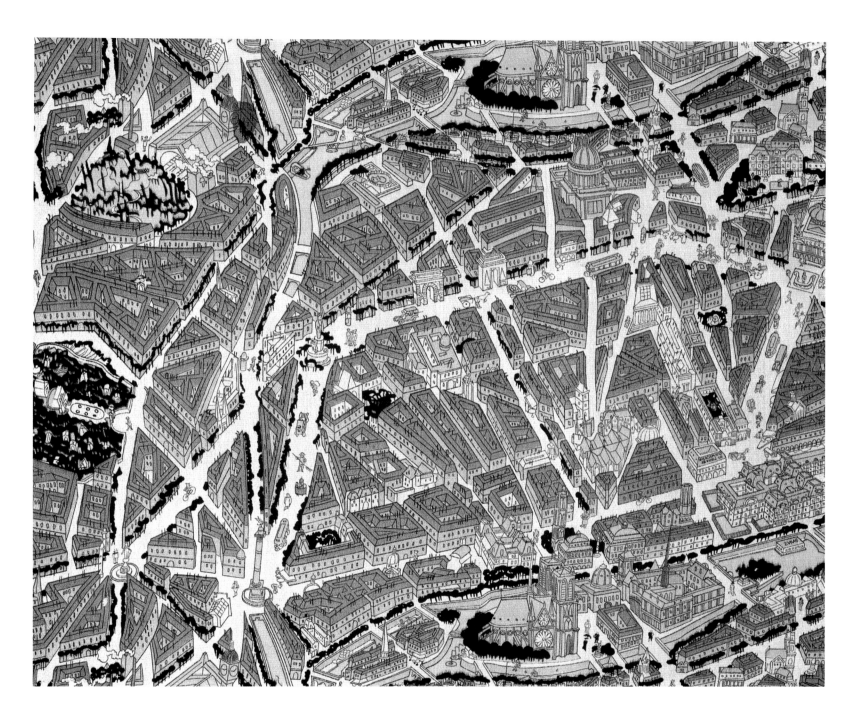

PLATE 63. *Map of Paris*, dress fabric. T.871-1930

PLATE 63. *Map of Paris*, dress fabric (detail). T.871-1930

85

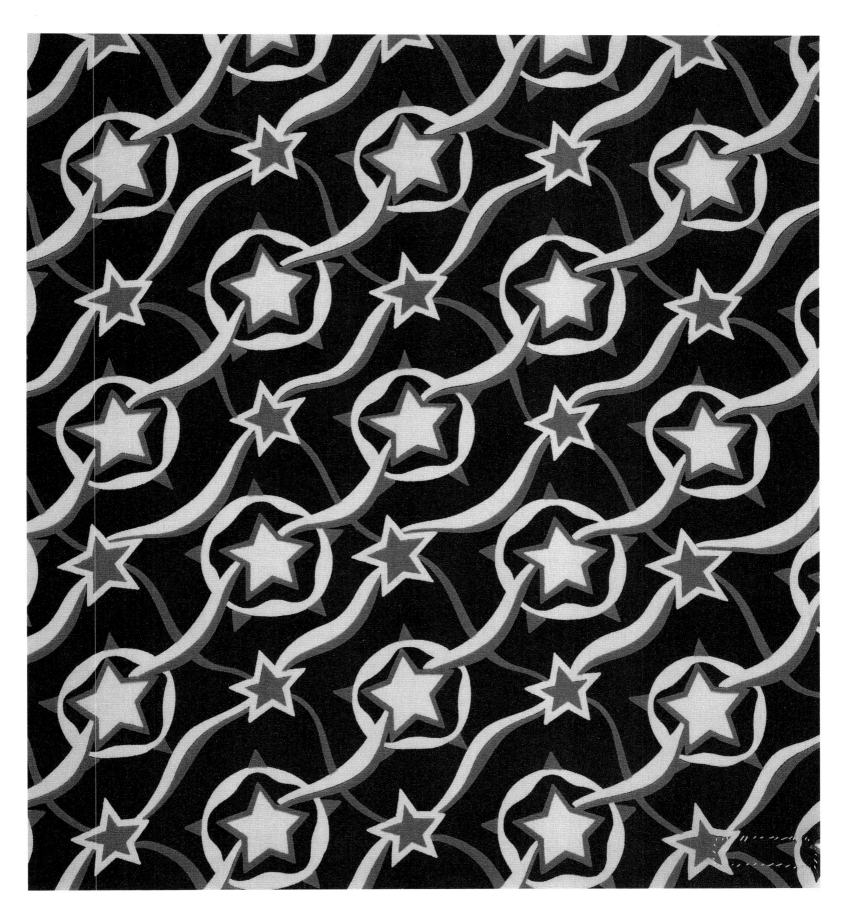

PLATE 64. *Stars and Stripes*, dress fabric. T.87E-1930

PLATE 65. *Gentlemen Prefer Blondes*, dress fabric. T.87L-1930

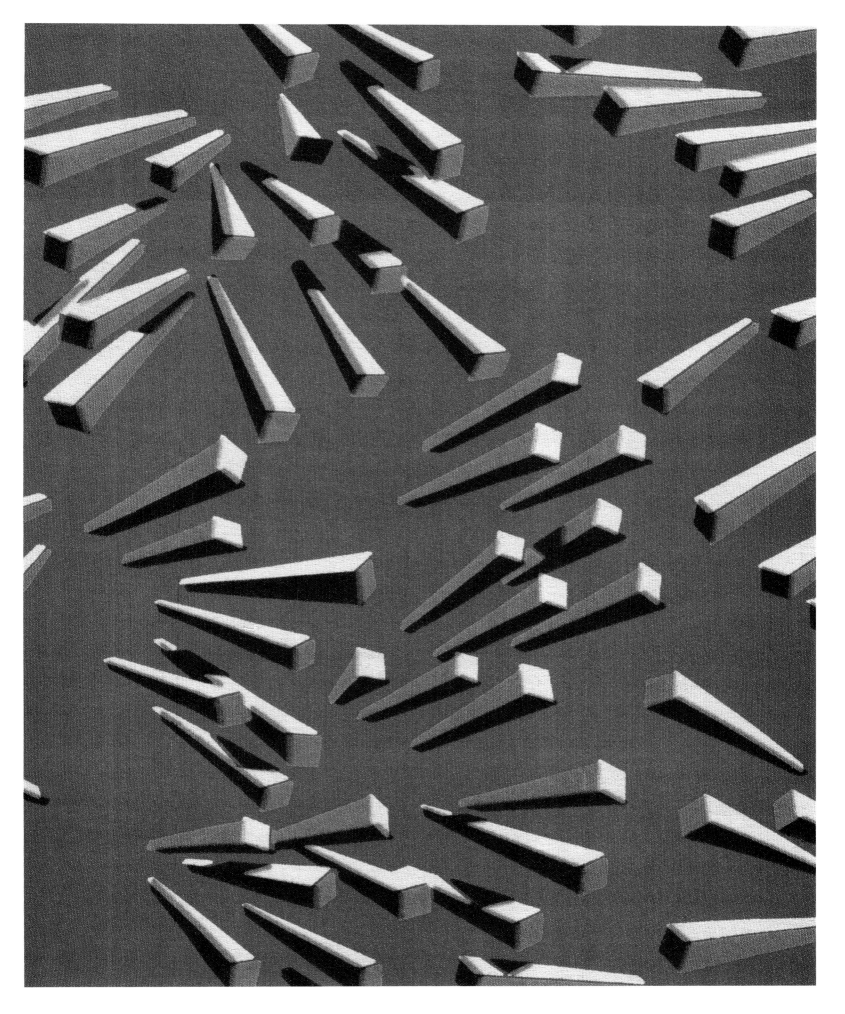

Plate 66. *Pegs*, dress fabric. T.87M-1930

PLATE 67. *Moth Balls and Sugar Cubes*, dress fabric. T.87P-1930

PLATE 68. Dress fabric. T.88C-1930

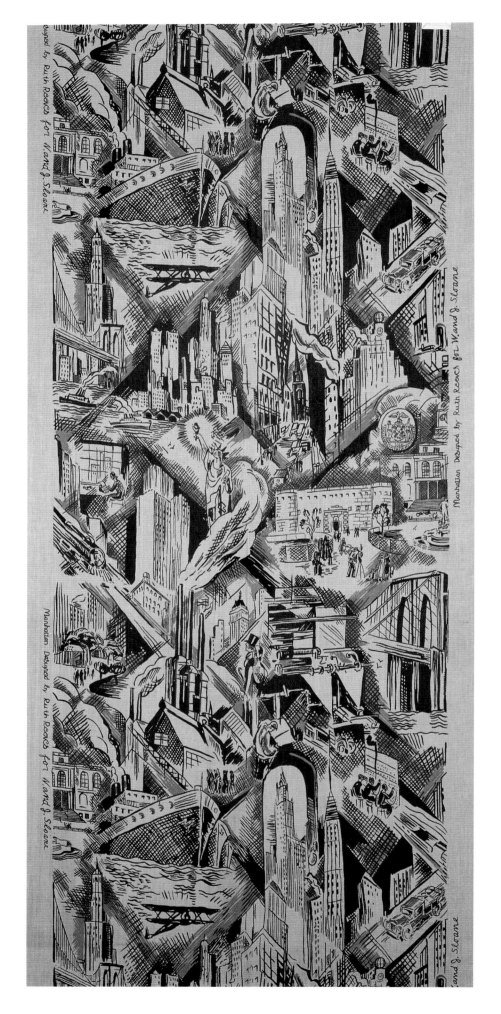

PLATE 69. *Manhattan*, hanging. T.57-1932

92

PLATE 70. *Homage to Emily Dickinson*, furnishing fabric. CIRC.282A-1932

PLATE 71. Hanging. T.56-1932

PLATE 72. *Essex Hunt*, furnishing fabric. T.58-1932

96

PLATE 73. *Play Boy*, printed cotton and monk's cloth. CIRC.276-1932

PLATE 73. *Play Boy*, printed cotton and monk's cloth (details). CIRC.276-1932

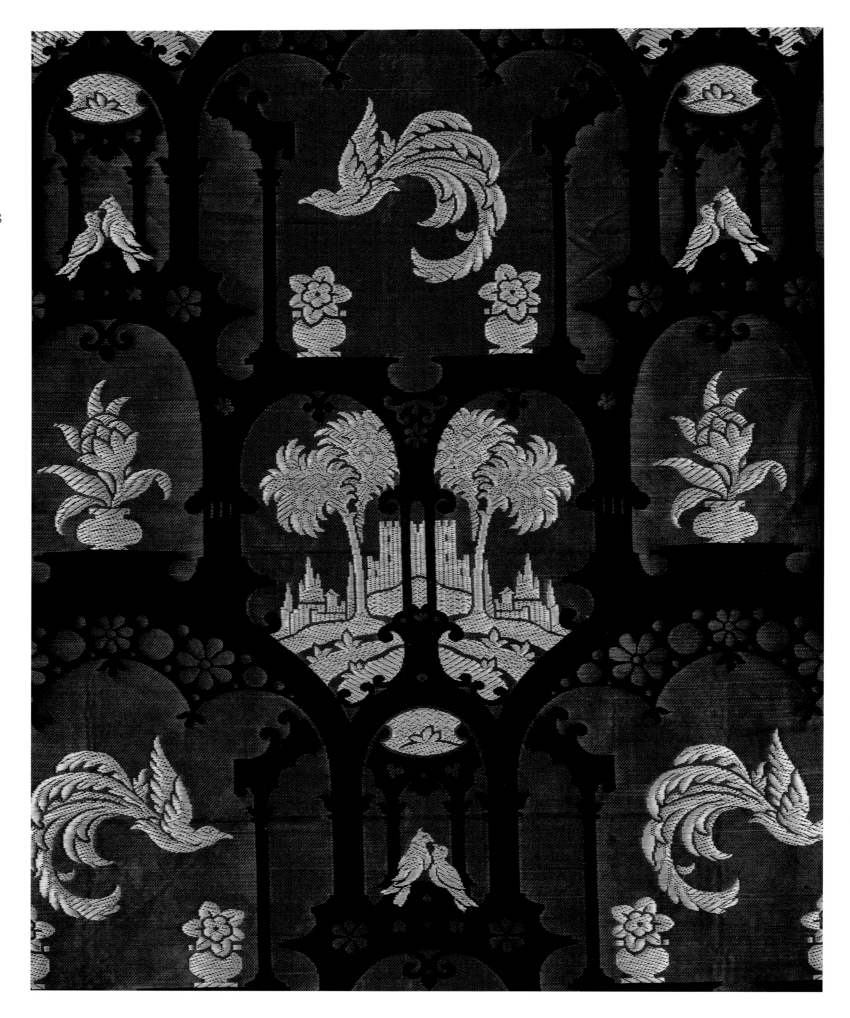

PLATE 74. *Teheran*, furnishing fabric. T.200-1972

PLATE 75. *Margery*, furnishing fabric. T.386B-1913

PLATE 76. *Grapes,* furnishing fabric. CIRC.236B-1935

PLATE 77. Furnishing fabric. CIRC.467-1966

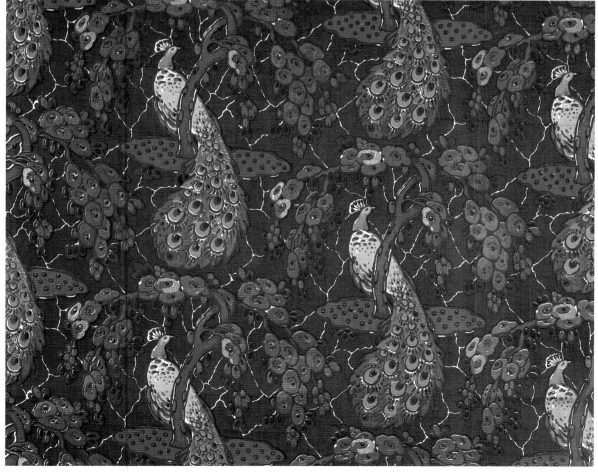

PLATE 78. Furnishing fabric. CIRC.454-1966

PLATE 78. Furnishing fabric (detail). CIRC.454-1966

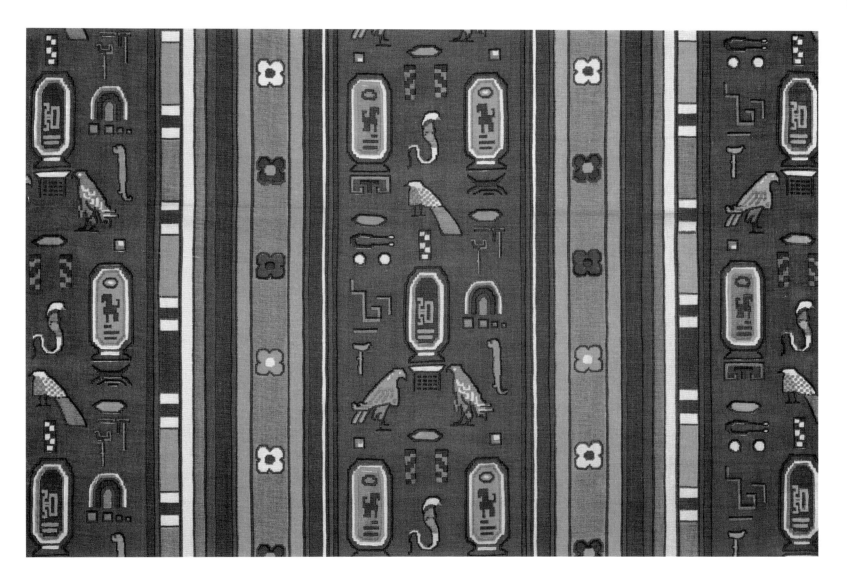

PLATE 79. Furnishing fabric. CIRC.668-1966

Plate 80. Furnishing fabric. Circ.613-1964

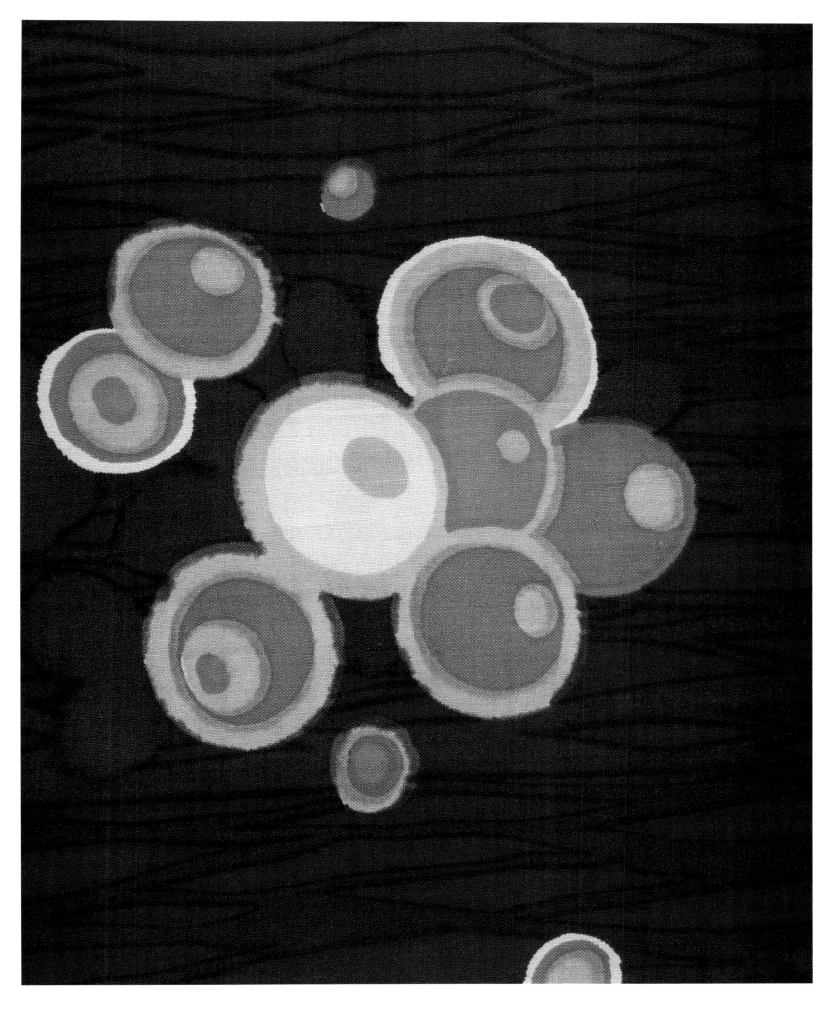

Plate 81. Furnishing fabric. Circ.441-1966

PLATE 82. Furnishing fabric. CIRC.447-1966

106

PLATE 83. Furnishing fabric. T.442-1934

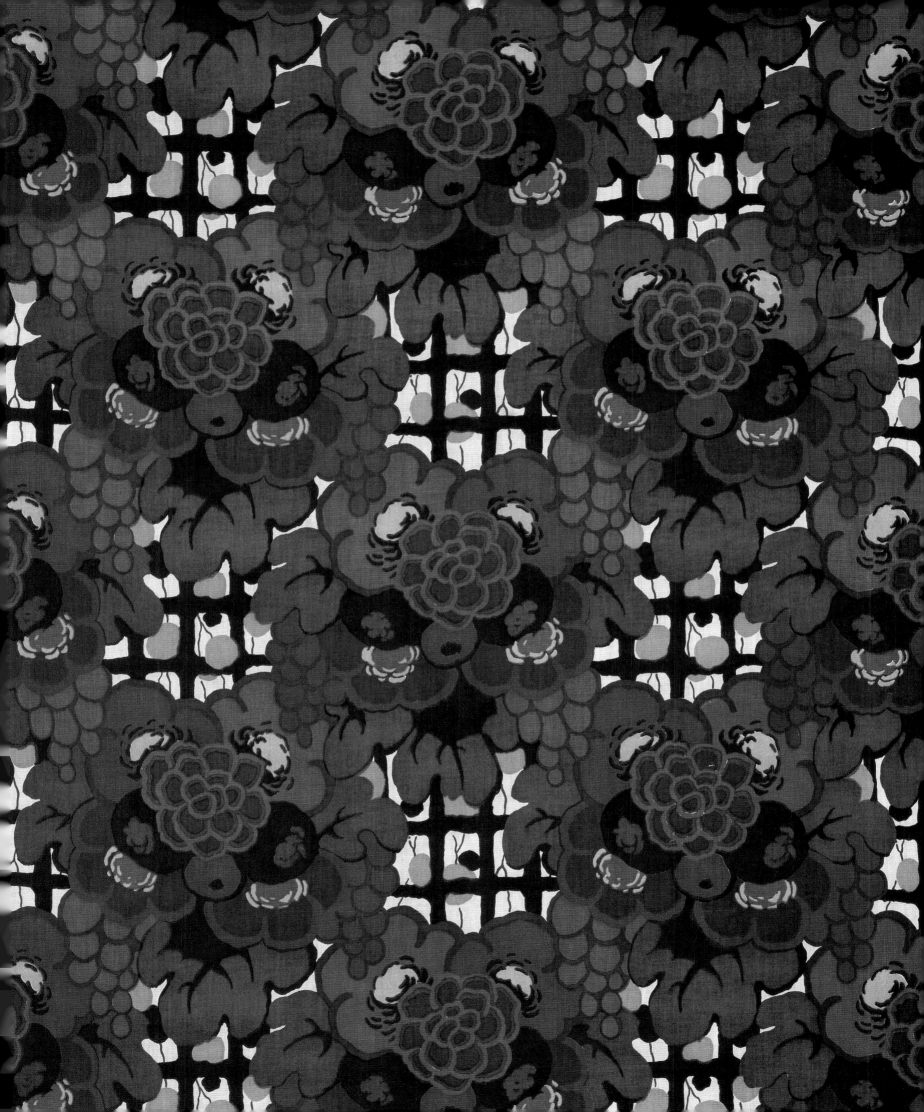

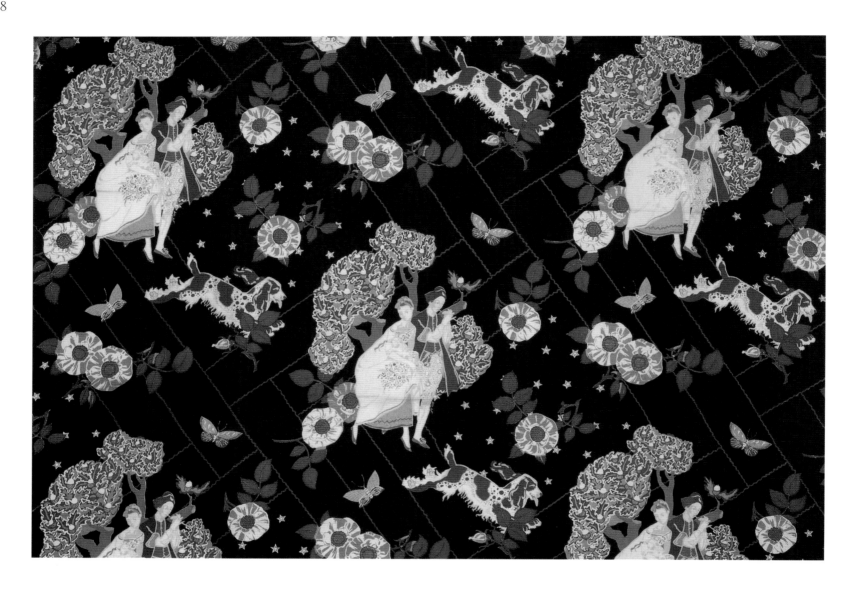

PLATE 84. Dress fabric. CIRC.475-1966

PLATE 84. Dress fabric (detail). CIRC.475-1966

PLATE 85. Furnishing fabric. CIRC.618-1964

PLATE 86. *Futurist*, furnishing fabric. T.16-1939

PLATE 87. Furnishing fabric, roller-printed cotton. CIRC.491-1966

PLATE 88. Furnishing fabric. T.100-1979

PLATE 89. Furnishing fabric. T.111-1979

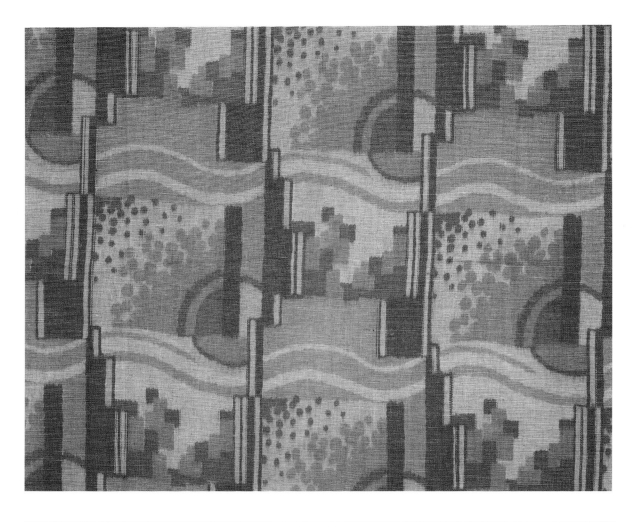

114

PLATE 90. Furnishing fabric. T.94-1979

PLATE 91. *Matelot*, dress fabric. T.244-1987

Plate 92. *Surfers*, dress fabric. T.264-1987

PLATE 93. Furnishing fabric. T.368-1934

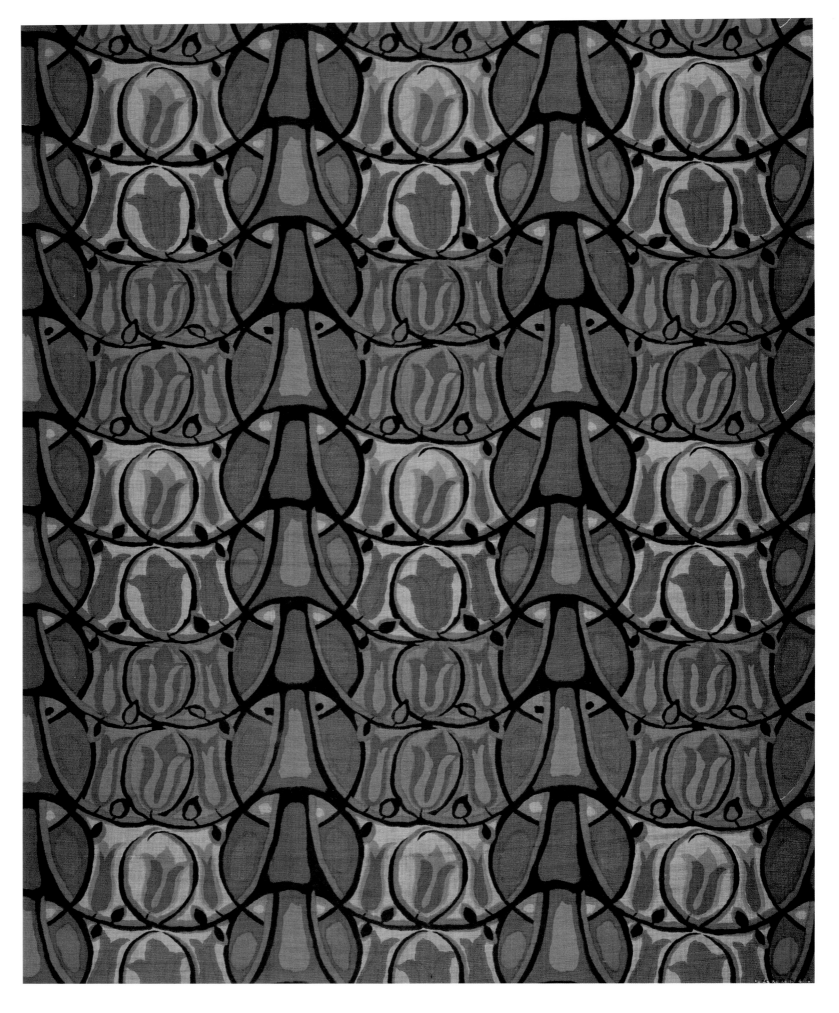

PLATE 94. Furnishing fabric. T.413-1934

PLATE 95. Furnishing fabric. T.400-1934

PLATE 95. Furnishing fabric (detail). T.400-1934

PLATE 96. Furnishing fabric. CIRC.630-1956

PLATE 97. Furnishing fabric. T.440-1934

PLATE 98. Furnishing fabric. CIRC.566-1966

123

PLATE 99. Furnishing fabric. T.325-1934

PLATE 100. Furnishing fabric. CIRC.623-1964

125

PLATE 101. Shawl (detail). T.112-1975

PLATE 102. Shawl. T.84-1964

PLATE 103. Furnishing fabric. T.439-1934

128

292265

PLATE 104. *Cornish Farm*, dress fabric. T.63-1979

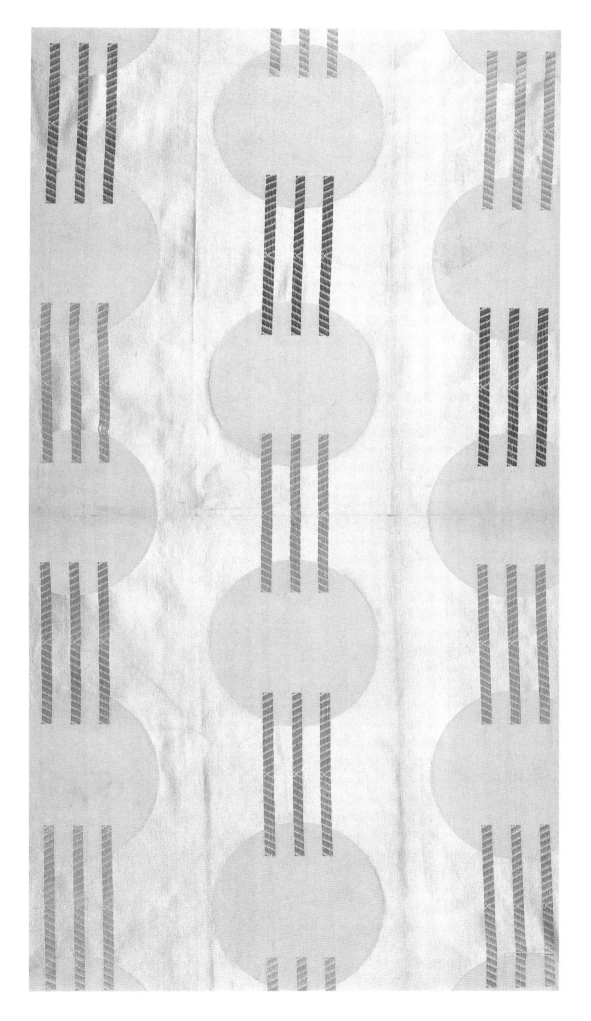

PLATE 105. *Disc*, furnishing fabric. T.203-1972

PLATE 106. Furnishing fabric. CIRC.805-1967

131

PLATE 107. Furnishing fabric. CIRC.804-1967

PLATE 108. *Avis*, furnishing fabric. CIRC.319C-1939

132

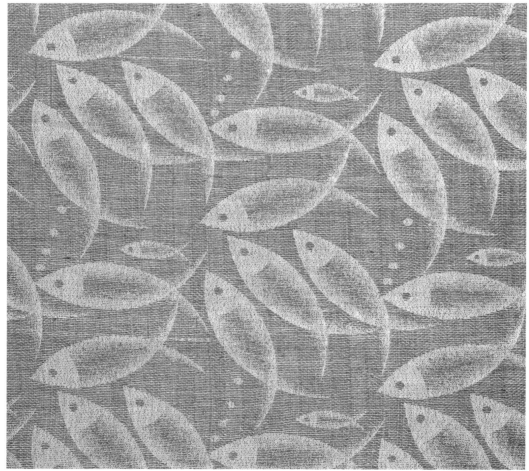

PLATE 109. *Mandalay*, furnishing fabric. CIRC.223-1935

Plate 110. Furnishing fabric. Circ.116-1937

Plate 111. Rug. Circ.480-1974

134

Plate 112. Rug. T.440-1971

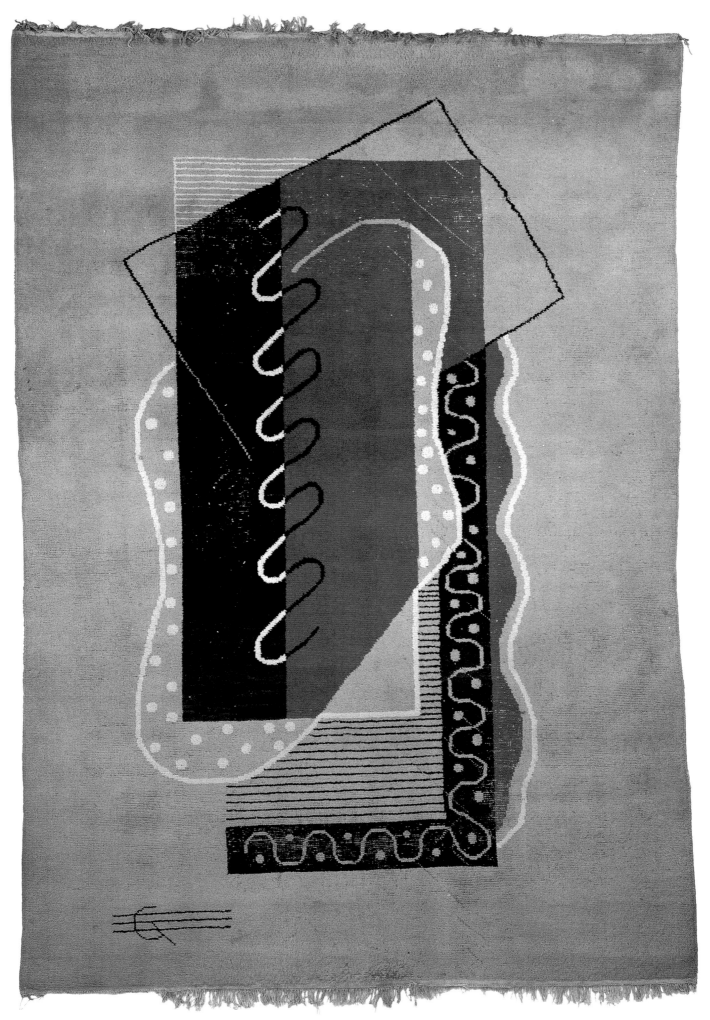

PLATE 113. Rug. T.440-1976

PLATE 114. Rug. T.296-1977

Plate 115. Rug. T.157-1978

Plate 116. Carpet. T.100-1999

GLOSSARY

ARTIFICIAL SILK See Rayon.

BATIK Discharge dye technique. Wax is applied to the textile to protect the patterned areas before it is submerged in the dye bath. The process can then be repeated by removing areas of wax and dyeing the exposed parts with further colours. Characterized by fine surface veining where the wax has cracked and permitted the dye to penetrate. Mass-production involves roller-printing the wax on to the fabric from heated rollers prior to dyeing. This handcraft, originating in Indonesia, became popular in the artistic centres of Europe during the 1920s.

BLOCK-PRINTING One of the oldest methods of printing. The pattern is cut in relief on wooden blocks, with a separate block for each colour to be printed. The colour is transferred from the block face to the surface of the cloth by hitting the back of the block with the handle of a mallet. It is a skilled, costly and labour-intensive process and was superseded in the twentieth century by mechanized roller- and screen-printing.

CUBISM The first purely abstract school of painting, founded by Picasso and Braque. Characterized by a shifting perspective rendered by a fractured representation of the subject. This revolutionary approach rejected the depiction of a unified space from a single viewpoint, which had been posited by artists since the Renaissance. Its representation of simultaneous, multiple views has been interpreted as the introduction of the concept of time and movement into painting, for traditionally a picture could capture only one instant. Cubist canvases were initially subdued and monotonous in colour, as their main purpose was to investigate forms in space.

EXPRESSIONISM Following on from Fauvism, the adherents of Expressionism sought to incite strong emotion through their painting. Characterized by vigorous brushwork, jarring colours and stark, flattened forms, Expressionism was closely associated with Kokoschka and Kandinsky, although it was primarily a German movement pioneered by such artists as Beckmann and Nolde.

FAUVISM A short-lived art movement whose followers employed vivid, discordant hues, simplified forms and a visible surface texture in an attempt to express emotion through painting. One of the first twentieth-century groups to be influenced by non-Western cultures. Matisse, Dérain and Dufy were all practitioners, and critics labelled them 'fauves', meaning 'wild beasts', for their supposed lack of restraint.

FUTURISM An Italian movement established in 1909 by the poet Marinetti. The Futurists embraced speed and technology in their manifesto as well as an anarchic rejection of their artistic heritage. Boccioni's sculptures and the paintings of Severini and Balla depicted figures in motion.

POCHOIR A hand-colouring technique that involves filling in the areas of a stencilled plate with watercolour or gouache. The resulting areas of compartmentalized colour are typical of the Art Deco style. Paul Iribe popularized the method when he used it to illustrate *Les robes de Paul Poiret racontées par Paul Iribe* (1908). It was subsequently taken up by many graphic artists, including the Frenchmen Séguy, Bénédictus and Georges Barbier as well as a number of Italian fashion illustrators of the 1920s and 1930s.

RAYON The name adopted to replace 'artificial silk' as the generic term for man-made fibres produced from a cellulose base. The two main types are viscose and acetate rayon. Viscose was patented in 1892 but rayon was developed for mass-production from about 1922–30. The versatility and durability of rayon yarn allow it to be made into a number of different fabrics or used in combination with natural fibres.

ROLLER-PRINTING This method, patented by Thomas Bell in 1783, was implemented on a large scale during the nineteenth and twentieth centuries. The design is engraved on copper rollers, one for each colour. The engraving is filled with colour and the cloth pressed on to it, while the rollers revolve around a central, stationary roller. The entire width of the cloth is printed. As the cost of engraving the rollers is high and large quantities of cloth have to be printed to recoup the initial outlay, roller-printing is usually reserved for best-selling designs. One machine can print thousands of yards in one day.

SCREEN-PRINTING The design is first drawn or photographically printed on to a celluloid sheet, then transferred on to a (silk) screen by applying light-sensitive gelatine to the screen, placing the celluloid sheet with the design on top of it and exposing them to light. Where light has reached the screen, the gelatine hardens and becomes insoluble. The remaining gelatine is washed away, leaving clear only the parts of the screen that carry the design. A separate screen is created for each colour.

Screen-printing became increasingly popular towards the end of the 1920s and during the 1930s. It proved an economical method for printing short runs of fabric, and was good for producing the broad effects which found favour later in the century. The early hand process has now largely given way to sophisticated fully automatic flat and rotary machine production.

TOILE DE JOUY A style of printed textile originating in late eighteenth-century France but inspired by indigenous Indian prints. Oberkampf, a German who owned a block-printing works based at Jouy near Versailles, invented a machine for printing fast colours on to cloth from engraved copper plates. The prints were often of neo-classical design, depicting scenes or tableaux framed by foliage.

WARP Yarns running the length of the cloth, usually stronger than the horizontal weft yarns.

WARP PRINT Fabric whose warp is printed prior to weaving. The parti-coloured threads are then interwoven with a monochrome weft. This breaks up the solidity of the colour mass and produces a soft, blurred outline. Such warp prints had a ready market in the early to mid-1930s.

WEFT Yarns that interlace at right angles with the warp.

Notes on Firms and Designers

BIANCHINI-FÉRIER, Lyons Large silk-weaving mill established in 1888 by the designer Charles Bianchini in partnership with François Férier, financier of the firm. It produced dress fabrics for Lanvin, Patou and Delaunay. During the 1920s the firm commissioned designs by artists including Georges Barbier, Robert Bonfils, Raoul Dufy and Alberto-Fabio Lorenzi.

BIIA British Institute of Industrial Art, founded in 1920 jointly by the Board of Trade and the Board of Education. Its purpose was very similar to that of the already existing DIA (see below): to exhibit contemporary work and encourage the exchange of ideas among designers. In 1922 the BIIA joined forces with the DIA although they retained their existing names. The BIIA was dissolved in 1934 and its collection given to the V&A. Many of the textiles donated to the Museum at this time are labelled with the initials of the Institute.

BONFILS, ROBERT (1886–1971) French artist-designer who worked in a number of different fields, including ceramics, fashion illustration for the *Gazette du Bon Ton* and book bindings. He also designed textiles for Bianchini-Férier and created the cover for the catalogue of the 1925 Exposition des Arts Décoratifs et Industriels Modernes.

CALICO PRINTERS' ASSOCIATION, Manchester An amalgamation of 46 British printing firms, several with spinning, weaving and dyeing plants, forming 85 per cent of the British calico-printing industry. It was established on 8 November, 1899.

CHAREAU, PIERRE (1883–1950) A French Modernist architect who created the striking Maison de Verre (1929), a combined clinic and home for a Parisian doctor featuring an extensive use of glass. He also designed furniture, particularly wood and metal pieces and light fittings. In 1928 he was a founding member of the Union des Artistes Modernes, a group at the forefront of 1930s design.

CHERMAYEFF, SERGE (1900–96) A Russian *émigré* living in England, he worked for the London decorating firm E. Williams and in 1928 became director of Waring & Gillow's Modern Art Studio, working with Paul Follot. As an architect, he joined the Mars Group and helped to popularize the Modernist style in buildings and interiors. He also worked with Erich Mendelsohn on the De La Warr Pavilion at Bexhill. In 1939 he emigrated to the US where he taught at Harvard and Yale, and continued his work as an architect.

DELAUNAY, SONIA (1885–1979) Russian *émigré* living in Paris. Together with her husband Robert Delaunay she experimented with Cubist paintings and explored associated theories in her dress and textile designs. She also created costumes and sets for the theatre and fashionable outfits trimmed with fur.

DIA The Design and Industries Association, founded in 1915 with the aim of improving the standards of British industrial design by exhibiting examples of the latest objects manufactured and propagating information about them to those working in the field.

DIM Maison de Décoration Intérieure Moderne An avant-garde French association of *ensembliers* founded by René Joubert in 1919.

DORN, MARION (1899–1964) Textile and carpet designer. Born and educated in San Francisco, she came to England in the early 1920s. By the mid-1930s she was generally acclaimed as a leading freelance textile designer, carrying out commissions for Claridge's, the Savoy and the ships *Orion*, *Orcades* and *Queen Mary*. In 1934 she founded her own firm, Marion Dorn Ltd, in New Bond Street. It was with difficulty, however, that she established herself in New York in 1940, and managed only moderate success in the US.

DUFY, RAOUL (1877–1953) Artist and textile designer who began his career making woodblock-printed book illustrations, then switched to fabrics for Poiret's Atelier Martine. From 1912 until 1930 he designed woven textiles for the silk manufacturers Bianchini-Férier, creating a range of distinctive and elegant fabrics, and was considered the foremost talent of his day. He continued to produce printed silk schemes for the Maison Onondaga in New York between 1930 and 1933, but gave this up to return to his original career as a painter.

EDINBURGH WEAVERS, Carlisle Experimental designing and marketing unit of Morton Sundour Fabrics Ltd. Established originally in Edinburgh in 1929, it was merged with the main weaving factory in 1930. Successfully directed by Alastair Morton, it issued avant-garde furnishings. It was taken over by Courtaulds in 1963.

L'Exposition Internationale des Arts Décoratifs et Industriels Modernes An exhibition held in Paris from April to October 1925 with the express aim of displaying cutting-edge decorative and industrial art, supposedly without reference to past design styles and methods. It occupied a vast site centred around the Pont Alexandre III and was a major showcase for French *ensembliers* and *artistes-décorateurs* of the day, establishing their supremacy in the field of interior design. It is also viewed, however, as the last flourishing of the 1920s taste for overt luxury, and the point at which Modernist, geometric forms began to come into their own. The descriptive label 'Art Deco', which encompasses the applied arts of the period from about 1910 to 1940, alludes to the name of this exhibition.

Follot, Paul (1877-1941) Furniture designer whose first pieces were in the Art Nouveau style but who adapted his work to suit the tastes of the 1920s. In 1923 he became director of the design studio Pomone attached to the Paris department store Au Bon Marché, and in 1928 collaborated with Serge Chermayeff at the Paris branch of the British store Waring & Gillow.

Foxton, William (1861–1945) Textile manufacturer who founded W. Foxton Ltd in 1903. The firm produced some of the most interesting artist-designed, printed and woven furnishings of the 1920s in London, commissioning artists such as Claude Lovat Fraser, F. Gregory Brown, Constance Irving and Minnie McLeish. Foxton was a founding member of the DIA, and on the governing council of the BIIA. Although no longer in the forefront during the 1930s, the firm continued to issue quality designs. Its records were destroyed during the Blitz.

Joel, Betty (1894–1985) Furniture and interior designer who established Betty Joel Ltd in Sloane Street shortly after the First World War with her husband David Joel. She designed carpets and textiles and showed furnishings by a range of designers at her later showroom in Knightsbridge. During the 1930s she made the furniture for a number of film sets.

Kauffer, Edward McKnight (1890–1954) Graphic artist and theatre designer, he was a fellow of the BIIA. Born and educated in the US, he trained as a painter and came to England in 1914 where he received important commissions for his graphic work. He illustrated a number of books and designed rugs for the Wilton Royal Carpet Factory.

Mackintosh, Charles Rennie (1868–1928) Architect, designer of furniture, metalwork and textiles, and watercolour painter. He trained at the Glasgow School of Art. His most famous buildings are the Glasgow School of Art, Miss Cranston's tearooms and Hill House. From 1916 until 1923 he lived in Chelsea and during these years designed many textiles, some of which were printed by W. Foxton Ltd and Sefton's.

Old Bleach Linen Company Ltd, Randalstown, Northern Ireland Linen manufacturers, bleachers and merchants. Established in 1870 by C.J. Webb. The company produced embroidery, dress and furnishing linens and published *The Embroideress*.

Poiret, Paul (1879–1944) After working with Doucet and Worth, Poiret became the most innovative dress designer of the 1910s, when he was inspired by the styles of the Orient to create fashions that dramatically changed the form and colouring of women's clothing. He dressed his models in loosely draped garments that were very different from the stiff, formal clothes of the time. His design studio, Atelier Martine, produced soft furnishings and textiles from 1912 until the 1930s, and he collaborated for several years with Raoul Dufy. By the 1920s clients perceived his style as too theatrical and he subsequently suffered financial difficulties and died bankrupt.

Reeves, Ruth (1892–1967) An American textile artist who trained with Fernand Léger during the 1920s and was influenced by his Cubist paintings. She produced a wide range of compositions for printed and woven fabric, many of which were manufactured by W. & J. Sloane of New York. One of her most acknowledged commissions was for the carpets in Radio City Music Hall.

Rodier, Lyons French weaving firm established by Paul Rodier, who had a reputation for creating eye-catching woven textures, usually in monochrome or subtle hues. The firm was best known for its fine woollen goods, including dress fabric with African motifs shown at the exhibition in Paris in 1925, and sheer cloth for curtains.

STEHLI SILKS CORPORATION, New York Firm producing dress silks, which commissioned the *Americana* range in the late 1920s from artists such as Ralph Barton, C.B. Falls, Edward Steichen, Dwight Taylor and Helen Wills.

STEINER, F. & CO. LTD, Church, near Accrington, Lancashire Dyers and calico printers founded by Frederick Steiner, who came to Britain in the early nineteenth century and took over Church printworks in the 1840s. High-quality printers, the firm used top designers and issued important Art Nouveau fabrics. It remained independent when many similar firms joined the CPA in 1899, but went into voluntary liquidation in 1955.

WALTON, ALLAN (1891–1948) Textile designer, manufacturer and interior decorator. He trained as both an architect and a painter. As director of Allan Walton Textiles, he commissioned some of the most enterprising artist-designed screen-printed fabrics of the 1930s. From 1943 to 1945 he was director of the Glasgow School of Art.

WARNER & SONS LTD, Braintree, Essex Leading nineteenth- and twentieth-century silk weavers and cotton printers. The firm was founded by Benjamin Warner. The first workshops were in Spitalfields, but the firm later transferred to Braintree Mills in Essex and is currently based in Milton Keynes. Warner was noted for high technical achievements and good design. It employed all the leading designers of furnishing and dress fabrics.

WIENER WERKSTÄTTE Founded in 1903 by Viennese architects Josef Hoffmann and Koloman Moser, this organization was intended to further the work and ideals of the Vienna Secession, especially the achievement of a total design concept, the *Gesamtkunstwerk*. Designers and craftsmen created a range of interior furnishings that were both hand-made and industrially manufactured. Eighty members of the textile department, which opened in 1910, produced about 18,000 designs, mainly for printed fabrics for furnishings and apparel, decorated primarily with stylized representations of the natural world. The overall design idiom attained an innovative degree of abstraction that was a seminal influence on Art Deco ornamentation.

WILTON ROYAL CARPET FACTORY LTD, Wilton, near Salisbury Carpet and rug manufacturer, established in the early eighteenth century. During the nineteenth century it was the leading producer of pile carpets, and worked under contract for Morris and Company. In 1934 it listed Wilton, Brussels and Axminster carpets as its specialities. During the 1930s the firm produced Wessex hand-tufted rugs, designed by leading artists.

BIBLIOGRAPHY

Arwas, Victor, *Art Deco*, Academy Editions, London, 1992

Battersby, Martin, *The Decorative Twenties*, Studio Vista, London, 1969; *The Decorative Thirties*, Studio Vista, London, 1969

Benoist, Luc, *Les Tissus, La Tapisserie, Les Tapis*, F. Rieder et cie, Paris, 1926

Bouillon, Jean-Paul, *Art Deco 1903–1940*, Editions d'Art Albert, Skira S.A., Geneva, 1989

Bowman, Sarah, *A Fashion for Extravagance: Art Deco Fabrics and Fashions*, Bell and Hyman, London, 1985

Boydell, Christine, *The Architect of Floors: modernism, art and Marion Dorn designs*, Mary Schoeser, Essex, published in association with the Architectural Library and the Royal Institute of British Architects, London, 1996

Damase, Jacques, *Sonia Delaunay: Rhythms and Colours*, Thames and Hudson, London, 1972

Delaunay, Sonia, *L'Art International D'Aujourd'hui 15: Tapis et Tissus*, Editions d'Art Charles Moreau, Paris, 1929

Duncan, Alistair, *American Art Deco*, Thames and Hudson, London, 1986; *Art Deco*, Thames and Hudson, London, 1988

Greenhalgh, Paul, ed., *Art Nouveau 1890–1914*, V&A Publications, London, 2000

Hawkins, Jennifer and Marianne Hollis, eds, *Thirties: British Art and Design Before the War*, Arts Council of Great Britain, London, 1979

Hayes Marshall, H.G., *British Textile Designers Today*, F. Lewis, Leigh-on-Sea, 1939

Herbst, René, *25 années: Union des arts modernes*, Editions du Salon des Arts Ménagers, Paris, 1956

Hillier, Bevis, *Art Deco of the 20s and 30s*, Studio Vista Limited, London, 1968

Hinchcliffe, Frances, *Thirties Floral Fabrics*, Webb & Bower, Devon, 1988

King, Donald, ed., *British Textile Design in the Victoria and Albert Museum*, Volume III, 'Victorian to Modern 1850–1940', Gakken Co. Ltd, Tokyo, 1980

Lambrechts, Marc, ed., *L'Art Déco en Europe: Tendances décoratives dans les arts appliqués vers 1925*, Les auteurs et la Société des Expositions du Palais des Beaux Arts, Brussels, 1989

van de Lemme, Arie, *Art Deco: An Illustrated Guide to the Decorative Style 1920–1940*, Grange Books, Kent, 1998

Lesieutre, A., *The Spirit and Splendour of Art Deco*, Paddington Press, New York, 1974

Moussinac, Léon, *Etoffes d'Ameublement Tissées at Brochées*, Editions Albert Lévy, Paris, 1926, *Etoffes Imprimées & Papiers Peints*, Editions Albert Lévy, Paris, 1924

Musée d'Art Moderne de la Ville de Paris, *Raoul Dufy Créateur d'Etoffes*, Paris, 1977

Possémé, Evelyne, *Le Mobilier Français 1910-1930: Les Années 25*, Editions Massin, Paris, 1999

Schoeser, Mary and Celia Rufey, *English and American Textiles from 1790 to the Present*, Thames and Hudson, London, 1989

Thieme, Otto Charles, *Avant Garde by the Yard*, Cincinnati Art Museum, Cincinnati, 1996

Tuchscherer, Jean-Michel, *Raoul Dufy Créateur d'Etoffes*, Imprimerie Brinkmann Mulhouse, Mulhouse, 1975

Verneuil, M. Pillard, *Exposition des arts décoratifs Paris 1925: Etoffes et tapis étrangers*, Editions Albert Levy, Paris, 1925

Völker, Angela, *Textiles of the Wiener Werkstätte 1910–1932*, Thames and Hudson, London, 1994